Time Management TRAINING

Lisa J. Downs

ASTD
PRESS

Alexandria, Virginia

ASTD Press is an internationally renowned source of insightful and practical information on workplace learning and performance topics, including training basics, evaluation and return-on-investment, instructional systems development, e-learning, leadership, and career development.

Ordering information: Books published by ASTD Press can be purchased by visiting our website at store.astd.org or by calling 800.628.2783 or 703.683.8100.

Library of Congress Control Number: 2007939265

ISBN-10: 1-56286-517-X
ISBN-13: 978-1-56286-517-7

ASTD Press Editorial Staff:
Director: Cat Russo
Manager, Acquisitions & Author Relations: Mark Morrow
Editorial Manager: Jacqueline Edlund-Braun
Senior Associate Editor: Tora Estep
Editorial Assistant: Maureen Soyars
Retail Trade Manager: Yelba Quinn
Editing and Production: Aptara Inc., Falls Church, VA, www.aptaracorp.com
Project Manager/Developmental Editor: Robin C. Bonner
Copyeditor: Ellen Newman
Indexer: Dorothy M. Jahoda
Proofreader: Sarah A. Bonner
Cover Design: Alizah Epstein
Cover Illustration: Frédéric Joos

Printed by Victor Graphics, Inc., Baltimore, Maryland, www.victorgraphics.com

The ASTD Trainer's WorkShop Series is designed to be a practical, hands-on road map to help you quickly develop training in key business areas. Each book in the series offers all the exercises, handouts, assessments, structured experiences, and ready-to-use presentations needed to develop effective training sessions. In addition to easy-to-use icons, each book in the series includes a companion website or CD-ROM with PowerPoint presentations and electronic copies of all supporting material featured in the book.

Contents

◆

◆

Remember when, as a child, it felt like time crept by painfully slowly? When it seemingly took *forever* for your birthday to come around again or that vacation from school would *never* arrive? My dad always told me that the older you get, the faster the time goes. I didn't believe him until I became an adult. How true it is! In my opinion, time is one of the most interesting phenomena in our lives, yet our experiences with it are all relative. How often in the last year have you or someone you know said, "There never seem to be enough hours in a day" or "I just don't have any time to myself anymore"? The crux of the issue is ensuring that we manage the time we have and that time does not manage us. Easier said than done, right?

So, why does it seem like we never have enough time and that many of us spend our days rushing around? After all, we have no more or less time than our ancestors, who toiled in the fields all day long. The answer lies in the events of our daily lives. With increased demands on our time from work, family life, technology, and other activities, it feels like our time is not our own. The key is to budget our time well, and then make the most of it. My hope is that you're able to take this book and use it to help others learn and apply strategies and tools to improve their time management and organizational skills, so they (and you!) can start to feel more in control and less stressed.

This book is organized in a way that allows trainers to easily focus their efforts on the needs of their learners and client organizations, and it provides practical exercises that walk participants through analyzing their own time management habits, learning a step-by-step process for time management, and practicing specific time management skills to use in a variety of situations. The training modules presented in the book challenge trainees to try strategies with which they may be unfamiliar in a context that encourages flexibility in a supportive learning environment. We have plenty of time; we just have to help each other use it most effectively for greater productivity and balance.

The chapters include a number of original and adapted structured experiences and instruments developed specifically for this book. Please feel free to adjust them to meet your needs and apply them to other aspects of your learning program. Many can be used for a wide range of training topics, such as supervisory skills, communication skills, personal productivity, and stress management. Some may already be familiar to you, as there are many effective foundational activities and models around time management that work so well that it's hard to imagine time management training without them.

Many thanks to Mark Morrow at ASTD Press for the opportunity to write this book and for his flexibility, guidance, and encouragement during the process. You are a delight to work with, and I appreciate your understanding and support. Thank you, as well, to Tora Estep at ASTD Press for managing this project, and to Robin Bonner and her team at Aptara Corporation for their professionalism and expertise in working through the editorial and composition processes.

Thank you to my friends, family, and learning and development colleagues with ASTD Puget Sound and beyond, who offered their support and enthusiasm for my writing adventures. Special thanks to my dear friends Ann Callister, Steve Shulze, and Tom Sulewski for their camaraderie, support, and laughter.

Finally, thank you to my husband, Chris, who lovingly tolerates my crazy life and who is a sea of calm in the midst of chaos.

Lisa J. Downs

Redmond, Washington

July 2008

◆

Introduction: How to Use This Book Effectively

What's in This Chapter?

- ◆ Practical definition of time management

- ◆ Common issues in teaching time management skills

- ◆ Explanation of how to use this workbook most effectively

What Is Time Management?

Time management is a way to develop and use processes and tools for maximum efficiency, effectiveness, and productivity. It involves mastery of a set of skills, such as assigning priorities for tasks, setting goals, scheduling, planning, and delegating. It is often necessary for an individual to experiment with various time management tools and methods to discover the blend of strategies that works best. At the heart of effective time management is the ability to take charge of the time we have.

Time management generally involves a five-step process: setting priorities, analyzing, filtering, scheduling, and executing. This process, which involves changing habits, uses a number of behaviors and tools to be most effective. Each step requires specific skills, and some people may move through the process more quickly than others. Various aspects of time management may be a challenge, such as how to handle email, procrastination, interruptions, and paperwork. Self-awareness plays a large part in effective time management. The facilitator of a time management workshop helps learners to recognize strengths and weaknesses in how they use their time and to develop strategies to increase their effectiveness.

For purposes of this workbook, *time management* is defined as effective use of time to achieve desired results.

Why This Is Important

Time management is a set of behaviors that may take many different forms for different people. The behaviors and tools used in one situation may not be the same as those used in another. This is an important point to emphasize when teaching effective time management. Although an effective time manager follows a process, and certain behaviors lead to success more often than others, learners may not use all of the techniques provided in a workshop. They may also use different strategies to improve their time management effectiveness, and this is perfectly acceptable. This book facilitates the accelerated development and effective delivery of training to prepare participants to improve their time management skills and overall productivity.

How the Book Was Developed

The author reviewed available literature on the subject of time management. She combined this knowledge with her extensive experience in teaching time management skills, as well as in the design and delivery of effective, interactive training for adult learners. A leader of numerous seminars in many aspects of management and communication, the author currently serves as a workshop facilitator and coach to help others improve their personal and professional effectiveness—a background that enriches the contents of this book.

The Context of the Training

The materials and designs in this book are appropriate for a wide range of organizations, both public and private. The training materials help participants become aware of their time management behaviors and then develop the skills necessary to be effective time managers. Although the book is designed to train people for individual time management scenarios, with little or no adjustment, many of the approaches and principles also apply to small- or large-group time management situations, such as with a workgroup or team.

The Content of the Training

The various aspects of time management, including the process, behaviors, tips, and recommended tools, will be new information for many learners. Some participants or organizations, however, may not consider time management to be a skill that requires much training. They may believe that if someone is not well organized, not much can be done about it. This viewpoint has made teaching time management more difficult for some trainers.

Another related issue is that some organizations lack the resources, particularly time, to offer this type of training. Other training topics, initiatives, or projects may take priority over effective individual time management. Clear identification and communication of the desired results of the training helps participants and others in the organization understand the benefits and skills taught during a time management workshop.

The training designs in this workbook are intended to address these concerns. The content modules in chapter 10 are divided into the basic skills required for effective time management, particularly ways of working through the process and handling specific barriers to being a good time manager.

BASIC SKILLS

- ◆ **Content Module 10–1: Participant Introductions.** To help create a collaborative learning environment, this module introduces participants to each other and suggests that their roles are to contribute to the learning process.

- ◆ **Content Module 10–2: Time Management Defined.** The phrase *time management* may be ambiguous for some people. This module clarifies what it means to manage time, the importance of recognizing good time management, and how to identify and avoid common time wasters.

- ◆ **Content Module 10–3: Time Management Self-Assessment.** This module helps participants assess their strengths and weaknesses in managing time, and it explores how poor time management can negatively affect our work with others, as well as individual productivity and efficiency.

- ◆ **Content Module 10–4: The Time Management Process.** A five-step process for effective time management is included in this module. It suggests ways to set priorities and analyze how time is currently being spent, and it offers strategies to filter information and handle the demands on our time.

- ◆ **Content Module 10–5: Goal-Setting.** This module explains techniques to set and achieve goals, including how to identify priorities to gain focus.

- ◆ **Content Module 10–6: Scheduling Time and Tasks.** This module helps participants understand some of the tools available for scheduling and tips to plan effectively when tasks will get done.

- ◆ **Content Module 10–7: Effective Delegation.** Positive and negative consequences of delegation are addressed in this module. Participants will explore the behaviors they currently exhibit and those they need to develop.

SKILLS TO HANDLE BARRIERS

- ◆ **Content Module 10–8: Procrastination.** This module explores the many traps of procrastinating behaviors and how to recognize them. Participants also get firsthand experience in dealing with some procrastination scenarios and strategies to overcome procrastinating self-talk.

- ◆ **Content Module 10–9: Interruptions and Distractions.** This module gives participants the opportunity to practice some techniques to handle common "time robbers," such as interruptions and other distractions.

- ◆ **Content Module 10–10: Managing Email.** One of the most common challenges in time management today, managing email can be a tough skill to master. This module focuses on how to successfully tackle email, especially in relation to other demands on our time.

- ◆ **Content Module 10–11: Working With Paperwork.** This module addresses a critical aspect of being a good time manager: how to handle paperwork and other clutter effectively as a way to be organized and efficient. It also includes a wrap-up activity to help participants focus on an organization action plan.

The Probable Realities of Participants

Most participants in a training course have common issues and common experiences. The needs-assessment process will provide specific information for a particular group of participants or for an organization. The following issues are present in many workshop situations, and it may help the trainer to be aware of them when designing and facilitating a training program on effective time management:

◆ **Participants may not want to be in the training workshop.** Some attendees do not want to sit in class and consider it to be a waste of time, particularly if the training topic is on the soft side. All or some of the participants may be required to attend the workshop as part of a mandatory curriculum.

◆ **Participants may not clearly understand the desired results of the training.** Lack of clarity about the benefits of attending a workshop on effective time management and the skills they will learn may negatively affect learners' participation.

◆ **Participants may not have had any training on how to be a good time manager.** Time management is often viewed as a naturally occurring skill. Although people are often told that they are well organized, "on top of things," or that they need to be better organized, the participants may be unclear about what that means and how to improve. It's a good sign that they are attending the workshop, but the participants may not have had any formal training on the topic prior to the program.

◆ **Some participants may not even have time to get organized.** Often, people see the skills they learn in a workshop as an addition to their normal tasks and activities. In particular, some may feel that it will take more time to set up processes, systems, and tools, and that this is time they just don't have, which is an interesting implication for a time management workshop. Although this could be the case, some participants may have trouble understanding how they can incorporate new learning into their lives.

◆ **Participants may perceive attending the training as a sign that they are highly deficient in time management skills.** If the training is mandatory for some participants, they may see this as an embarrassment based on their time management skill level. Although this perception may or may not be true, some view training as a remedial activity rather than one designed to enhance personal and professional effectiveness. This may affect participation in training exercises.

- **Participants come into the training with marked differences in their skill and knowledge levels.** In a single workshop, participants may come from all levels in the organization's hierarchy with varying degrees of knowledge, skill, and experience. Those at the high end of the spectrum may think the workshop is not aligned with their experience level, and those at the lower level may be intimidated to be in the same training as their supervisors or senior management.

- **Participants may not have any clear incentive to improve their time management skills.** Some training attendees may not be internally motivated to develop their time management skills further; no consequence, such as a negative score on a performance measure, may exist to encourage participation. In these situations, the trainer may face resistance to participation in workshop activities or large-group discussion.

- **The need to manage time effectively may be tied to increasing customer satisfaction.** For many participants, improving their time management skills may affect their relationships with their clients or customers, in turn leading to referrals and to increases in status or compensation.

- **The participants have received a specific directive to improve their time management skills.** Some participants may attend the training session to learn skills to address specific situations or issues with their time management. Although this could easily enhance the workshop, participants may attempt to steer discussion and activities toward helping them resolve a particular issue, which may inhibit the learning experience for others.

- **Participants may need to deal with competing interests during the training.** Whether it is checking voicemail, handling email, or dealing with an urgent client issue, some participants may not fully attend the workshop or may attempt to multitask during the time management skills training, another interesting implication for a time management workshop. This may affect the learning environment, the effectiveness of training activities, and the workshop experiences of others.

How to Use This Book

The best use of this resource is to develop and conduct training sessions on the subject of improving the time management skills of learners. Both experienced and novice trainers will be able to use this book in a flexible manner to ensure that their sessions meet the real needs of their client organizations.

Sample training designs are included in this book, along with the materials they require. The individual content modules, structured experiences, assessments, and training instruments in this book can be incorporated into training already offered; they can also be mixed and matched into a variety of custom designs.

The author strongly suggests that you

- ◆ Identify your target audience for effective time management training

- ◆ Assess the learning needs of potential participants

- ◆ Modify the enclosed designs, if necessary, or develop new ones

- ◆ Evaluate the outcomes of the participants' training sessions for continuous improvement of the trainer and the training sessions.

This book can be a reference from which you borrow the structured experiences, instruments, assessments, and designs that fit your specific needs. A comprehensive set of steps that can help you get the most value out of this book appears at the end of each chapter under the heading "What to Do Next."

The Book's Organization

This resource contains numerous individual items that can be combined in many training designs for learners, including these major sets of materials:

- ◆ **Methods and effective practices** to assess the learning needs of actual or potential participants (chapter 2).

- ◆ **Evaluation methods and effective practices** for time management training sessions, including assessment of the trainer and continuous improvement approaches (chapter 5).

- ◆ **Content modules** that are either ready to use as is or that can be modified to meet specific needs (chapter 10).

◆ **Assessments and training instruments** that address several vital dimensions of time management effectiveness (chapter 11 and website).

◆ **Structured experiences** on a variety of topics relevant to effective time management training (chapter 12 and website).

◆ **Microsoft Word documents** to assist in customizing the participant manuals (website).

◆ **Microsoft PowerPoint presentations** to help trainers make presentations and give instructions (website).

◆ **Bibliography** of additional resources that can support time management training.

The goals of this book are to instruct and equip trainers with the tools to design and conduct highly interactive, engaging time management training for learners that is clearly on target.

Icons

 Assessment: Appears when an agenda or learning activity includes an assessment, and it identifies each assessment presented website.

 Website: Indicates materials included on the website accompanying this workbook.

DOWNLOADS

 Clock: Indicates recommended timeframes for specific activities.

 Discussion Questions: Suggests questions you can use to explore significant aspects of the training.

 Handout: Indicates handouts that you can print or copy and use to support training activities.

 **Key Point:** Alerts you to key points that you should emphasize as part of a training activity.

PowerPoint Slide: Indicates PowerPoint presentations and slides that can be used individually. These presentations and slides are on the website linked to this workbook, and copies of the slides are shown at the end of chapter 9. Instructions for using PowerPoint slides and the website are included in the appendix.

Structured Experience: Introduces structured experiences (participant exercises), which are included in chapter 12.

Training Instrument: Identifies specific tools, checklists, and assessments that are used before, during, and after the training workshop.

What to Do Next: Highlights recommended actions that you can take to make the transition from one section of this workbook to the next or from a specific training activity to another within a training module.

What to Do Next

◆ Study the entire contents of the book to get an overview of the resources it contains.

◆ Review the contents of the accompanying website so that you can understand how it relates to the material in the printed book. Open the files in Microsoft Word, PowerPoint, and Adobe Acrobat Reader so you are able to determine how to make copies of the forms you will need to print and the presentations you may use to enrich the material. This step should include a careful reading of the Appendix, "Using the Website."

◆ Study and apply the strategies outlined in chapter 2, "Assessing the Needs of Learners," to ensure that your sessions with learners are relevant and timely.

◆ When you have absorbed the information you discover in your training needs assessment, proceed to chapter 3. Design your session to meet the specific learning needs your potential participants have expressed. Carefully consider modifying the designs in this book as you formulate your plan to facilitate the learning of your client audience. Sample designs in chapters 6 through 9 can be used or modified as your needs analysis suggests. The content modules in chapter 10 are detailed. You can plan to facilitate them as they are or adapt them. Chapters 11 and 12 contain the structured experiences, assessments, and training instruments the modules require. Each of these is also a stand-alone item, so you can easily incorporate any or all of them into your existing training designs.

◆ Prepare to facilitate your training by studying the approaches in chapter 4. Each of your sessions should improve on the previous ones, and that chapter contains tips on how you can make sure that you gain knowledge along with your trainees. You will learn to become a highly effective facilitator, and the trainees will learn to become highly effective time managers.

◆ Plan to evaluate each of your training sessions. Chapter 5 tells you why this is important and gives you steps to gain insight into the payoffs of your time management training. Outline the steps you will take to gather and analyze evaluation data, and modify your training design as a result.

◆

Assessing the Needs of Learners

What's in This Chapter?

- ◆ Methods for needs assessment

- ◆ Tips to improve your assessment

- ◆ How to use two key assessment tools

- ◆ Guidelines for conducting successful focus groups

Assessment Steps

A training needs assessment identifies how training can meet the needs of both an organization and its learners. As the foundation for a successful training program, the needs assessment supports employee performance; its ultimate goal is to add value to meet an organization's business needs. Here are the steps necessary to conduct a needs assessment:

- ◆ **Identify the business needs of the organization and determine its culture.** A needs assessment will help determine whether a time management skills workshop is indeed a solution or if there is some other underlying performance issue present. An organization may sometimes view training as a panacea to cure all ills; if so, an assessment will reveal this information. Ask such questions as: What business strategies would a time management training support? Are there business problems that time management training could help solve? Is there data that may provide insight into this business need? What measures will be used to determine whether the training has had an impact on the business?

◆ **Identify the performance and learner needs.** It is important to know which behaviors must change to determine whether time management training is the appropriate solution. Data regarding the current and required performance of each potential learner, as well as the current and required skill and knowledge levels, will be helpful during this step in the needs-assessment process. Ask such questions as: What does the learner need to stop doing or start doing differently? How would you currently rate the learner in terms of effective time management, and how does this compare with what it should be? What knowledge and skills should the employee learn to be an effective time manager? What are the learning styles of potential participants?

◆ **Analyze the data.** The data collected will reveal whether a time management workshop should be recommended, as well as who should be included in the training. Look at any gaps in performance, knowledge, and skills, and determine the best candidates for the training based on the needs of the learners and the organization.

◆ **Deliver recommendations.** Present the findings of the assessment, including training and nontraining recommendations (such as processes and procedures, environment, and accountability). Share information regarding how the success of time management training will be measured, how the training will be designed and delivered, and how the program will be evaluated.

These methods and tools can help you complete the assessment process.

Methods

Many strategies exist to determine what potential training participants need to learn. Some are more time consuming than others, but here are five that are used frequently:

◆ **Existing data.** This can include benchmarking reports, performance appraisals, strategic plans, competency models, financial reports, job descriptions, mission statements, and annual reports. The advantage of this method is that it is readily accessible from the organization and provides hard, reliable data and measures. Because this information is typically gathered for purposes other than training, it is necessary to make inferences from the information to determine whether training issues are present.

◆ **Surveys.** This is usually an inexpensive way for respondents to provide information quickly and easily, either via an electronic tool or a paper-and-pencil questionnaire. Participants are asked a series of focused questions and are typically given a deadline by which to respond. Results are easy to tally and to analyze. It is important, however, to word the questions carefully so you get the required data, and so the questions also mean the same thing to each respondent.

◆ **Interviews.** One-on-one discussions, either in person or over the phone, can be used to gather individual learner and business needs data. Plan the interview questions ahead, record the session (with the interviewee's permission), and take notes. Although this is a time-consuming method, it can provide great detail and draw out information that is difficult to obtain from a survey. The interviewer must record responses objectively and not add his or her interpretation to what is said.

◆ **Focus groups.** In this data-collection method, conducting a group interview can provide information about learners' skill and performance levels, the work environment, culture, and perceptions of potential training participants. An advantage to focus groups is that all participants can hear each other and build on each other's ideas. Because this method can also be time consuming, it may be beneficial to have more than one facilitator conduct a focus group session.

◆ **Observation.** In this method, the observer visits the organization to watch learners perform their jobs and records information about behavior patterns, task performance, interactions with others, and use of time. Although this is helpful to assess training needs and skill levels for individual learners, the observer cannot record the mental processes of the learners. Another disadvantage is that individuals may behave differently around an observer than they would under normal circumstances.

Assessment Tips

Assessing the needs of learners should be carried out in a respectful, thoughtful way. Here are some tips that may help:

◆ **Gather the data that is going to provide an accurate and thorough assessment.** Discuss with the client what will be involved in conducting a needs assessment, as well as the approach taken to gain buy-in. Be sure to collect the data that will best address the learners' and the organization's needs regarding time management training, and go to the source(s) that will be able to provide the most accurate, pertinent information.

◆ **Focus only on the training and nontraining needs you can provide.** A needs assessment can be a reflection of your competency, so be sure that you are able to deliver on all solutions that arise from assessment results, whether it is time management training, coaching, or helping to fix a breakdown in a process. Trainers must be competent in a variety of learning and performance areas to conduct a thorough needs assessment for an organization. It is also in the best interest of the client to offer more than just a workshop as a possible solution to a performance or business issue.

◆ **Involve learners directly.** Ask learners about their needs through an interview, survey, or other assessment method to gather important data and gain buy-in from potential training participants. This simple way to determine the learners' preferred learning styles, previous experience with time management training, skill level, and what they would like to learn in an effective time management workshop will enhance the design and delivery of the training; it will also signal to the learners that they have a direct influence on the content and activities in a training session.

◆ **Use a variety of data-collection methods.** Use two or three methods to ensure that the correct solution will become apparent and that the needs of the clients and learners will be met. This also helps avoid analysis paralysis and the possibility of getting bogged down by too many tools and too much information. The use of different methods will also help maintain reliability and objectivity throughout the needs assessment process.

◆ **Present information free of trainer jargon.** Make an effort to address decision makers in language that is familiar to them rather than in trainer or performance improvement jargon that may confuse or alienate them. As with other professions, the field of learning and development contains its own acronyms and language that others may not understand. Stick to a discussion of success, impact on business issues, strategy, and learner needs.

Two Key Resources

Chapter 11 of this workbook contains two useful tools that trainers can use to assess the developmental needs of learners. Adapt either or both of these according to the client's requirements:

- ◆ **Assessment 11–1: Learning Needs Assessment Sheet.** This tool follows the steps in conducting a needs assessment and is designed to help you record information obtained by using the interview method of data collection. Adapt this form as needed. The Microsoft Word file is included on the website that accompanies this workbook.

- ◆ **Assessment 11–2: Time Management Self-Assessment.** Use this assessment as either a training tool or prework for a time management training session. You may also adapt the instrument for 360-degree assessments. Edit the Word file on the website that accompanies this workbook.

Using Focus Groups in Training Needs Assessment

Because conducting a focus group takes additional planning and can be more complex to facilitate than the other data collection methods, what follows is some detailed information on how to conduct a successful focus group session that may be helpful. A focus group is an efficient method for gathering data on the learners' needs for a time management training session. It is best to have at least two facilitators conduct the focus group: One should lead the session and keep the group on track, and the other should record the information from the session. The facilitators may want to alternate performing the roles of facilitator and recorder, depending on the length of the session and their abilities. It's a good idea to have an agenda for the session and to watch the clock. Because participants may go off on tangents or begin to complain about a variety of subjects, it will be important to stick to a plan and monitor the flow of conversation. It is also difficult to capture information when participants speak quickly, so it may be best to use audio or other equipment to record the conversation.

Here is a step-by-step process you can adapt to prepare for and conduct effective focus group sessions to assess the needs of learners:

- ◆ Determine the audience for time management training, and collect the contact information for each person.

- ◆ Schedule, well in advance, one or two focus group sessions in private, easily accessible facilities. Allow at least an hour for each session.

- ◆ Invite the members of the target audience to attend one or more focus groups to discuss what they would like to gain from time management training, how improved time management could benefit productivity in the organization, and the efficiency and productivity challenges they face. Limit the group size to five or seven members to encourage participants to speak freely and to be able to manage and take notes on the conversation.

- ◆ Print sufficient copies of Assessment 11–3: "Needs-Assessment Discussion Form" in chapter 11 and bring along extra supplies (such as pens, pencils, and notepads) for the participants.

- ◆ As the focus group begins, greet and welcome each person. Introduce yourself and ask the participants to introduce themselves by sharing the following information. You may want to write this list on a flipchart or whiteboard:

  - ◆ Name

  - ◆ Job title

  - ◆ Length of service at the organization

  - ◆ How they would currently rate their time management skills on a scale from 1 to 10

  - ◆ What their biggest challenge is when managing their time.

- ◆ Share with the participants the purpose of the needs assessment, how the data will be used, and why you were chosen to conduct the assessment. Ask their permission to record the focus group session.

- ◆ Hand out copies of Assessment 11–3: "Needs Assessment Discussion Form" and ask the participants to complete it candidly. Be sure they do not put their names on the forms, and explain that you will collect the sheets after the session.

- ◆ Ask the participants if they need more time, and, when ready, explain that they can make changes on the form during the discussion if they wish.

◆ Ask each person in the room the first question on the form. Be sure that you understand what each person says, and don't be afraid to ask for clarification, probe for specifics, or ask for examples. It is also a good idea to paraphrase responses for the other members of the group. Encourage participants to share what they have in common in response to the question.

◆ Facilitate the group's discussion through the remaining questions on the form. Start with a different participant each time, and intervene if necessary if one group member starts to dominate the discussion.

◆ Summarize the common themes and ideas that came out of the discussion with the participants, and verify the accuracy of what they said.

◆ Collect the participants' discussion forms, and remind them that the information will be used to help determine the content and activities for effective time management training that they will be invited to attend. If the training has been scheduled, share this information with the participants.

◆ Thank the focus group members for their participation.

What to Do Next

◆ Follow the Assessment Steps outlined at the beginning of the chapter to determine how you will go about conducting a needs assessment for your training.

◆ Decide the most effective method(s) to use for your needs assessment to gather pertinent data from key stakeholders.

◆ Determine who will need to be involved in the assessment process and arrange any necessary interviews or focus group sessions.

◆ Choose the (available) assessment tools you will use to help you carry out your needs assessment.

◆

Designing
Interactive Training

- Basic principles of adult learning

- Ideas for creating successful training sessions

- Training design tips

Principles of Design in Adult Learning

Good design is the essence of effective time management training, and it is a critical part of meeting the needs of learners and the client organization. Careful thought about the readiness, learning styles, and training needs of potential workshop participants will help to create an effective sequence of events to ensure that people will learn what is required in the allotted timeframe. The facilitator must have a structured plan to help learners develop the knowledge, skills, techniques, and attitudes they need to be successful. A solid training design makes the trainer more comfortable, which enables him or her to deliver an effective program that capitalizes on the facilitator's strengths and abilities as it addresses the participants' needs.

Malcolm Knowles (1998) has long been considered the father of adult learning and was the first to popularize the term *andragogy* to refer to the science of teaching adults. As a result of his thorough research about how adults learn, he made several assumptions about adult learning that affect how training is designed. Here is a list of those principles and the implications for time management training design:

- Adults need to know why they must learn something before they learn it. It is therefore the facilitator's responsibility to explain why the learning is of value and how the training will help the participants improve their time management skills.

◆ Adults need to be seen and treated as capable of making their own decisions and directing their own lives. As a result, they may liken training to their school experiences and resist participation. Trainers must make an effort to create learning experiences that help adults make the transition from dependent to independent learners by providing them with useful strategies and tools.

◆ The richest resources for adult learning are in the learners themselves, as they all have unique experiences to share. Adults have varied backgrounds, motivations, learning styles, interests, and needs, and it will be most effective for the facilitator to use the participants' experiences with time management and organization techniques during the training session.

◆ Learning must be authentic, as adults come ready to learn to cope with real-life situations. The learning should therefore coincide with a participant's development and be appropriate for the learner's skill and knowledge levels. To ensure that the training meets the needs of all learners, facilitators can use varied structured experiences and can share information that gets at the core of time management and personal productivity issues.

◆ Adults are motivated to learn if they believe the training will help them on the job and in their relationships. The most effective training helps individuals perform tasks and handle problems they confront in their everyday lives. Participants in a time management training session should be allowed to influence the learning approach, and the facilitator should use interactive training methods that focus on how they can apply the learning and change their behavior.

◆ The most potent motivators for adults are internal pressures: quality-of-life issues, job satisfaction, or respect in the workplace. Each person's type and level of motivation is different, so it is up to the trainer to identify what those motivators are for learners and decide how best to incorporate them into the training, which can be challenging.

Adult learners are also goal-oriented and are traditionally pressed for time with a finite capacity to absorb information. Limit lecture time for delivering information to allow a free exchange of ideas, and vary the presentation. This will also provide an engaging environment and ensure that different learning

Figure 3.1 Adult Learning in Practice

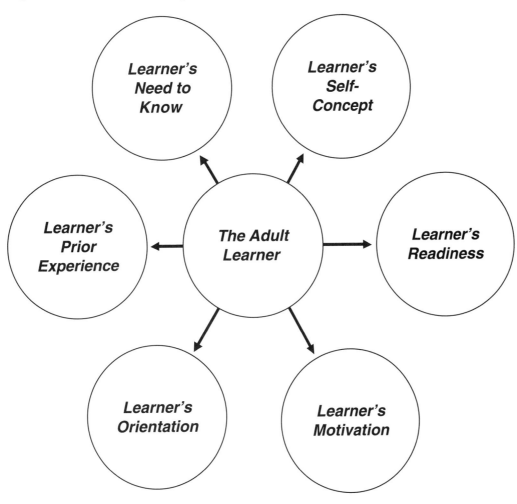

Source: Knowles, Malcolm S., Elwood F. Holton III, and Richard A. Swanson. *The Adult Learner* (5th edition). Houston, Texas: Gulf Publishing Company, 1998.

styles are taken into consideration. Give participants frequent breaks during a lengthy training session so they have opportunities to attend to their needs and get a mental break.

Figure 3.1 is a visual representation of Malcolm Knowles's elements of the adult learning model.

A Note on Training Language

The information about adult learning principles and the implications for designing effective time management training should make it clear that training is not teaching. Facilitators should not use language associated with education. For each word below, facilitators should substitute the training language in parentheses:

- ◆ Course (training session)

- ◆ Instructor (facilitator)

- ◆ Evaluation (assessment)

- ◆ Classroom (training room, facility, or venue)

- ◆ Textbook (participant manual or guide).

The organizational learning experience differs greatly from most academic experiences and is more targeted and practical. Many people have negative memories of their formal schooling, so trainers should be careful to avoid such reminders when they design training.

Using the Sample Designs in This Book

If you study the sample designs in chapters 6 through 9 and the content modules in chapter 10, you will discover a number of effective practices in designing interactive training for successful time management. Here are the major generalizations you may make in reviewing this material:

- ◆ **Break up the training into segments.** Determine the chunks of time you have, such as a half day or full day.

- ◆ **Break each major segment into smaller chunks.** Design each chunk so it has a beginning, middle, and end, and structure the length of each segment according to the time required for each activity. Be sure to consider participant breaks, time to get organized, and time for the facilitator to refresh himself or herself.

- ◆ **Anticipate which training activities may take more or less time than expected.** It is always better to plan too much than not enough, but you may need to adjust the timing of structured experiences depending on the participation level of the learners. If an activity takes more or less time than anticipated, prepare to adjust the timing of your remaining activities or insert another one on the spot.

- ◆ **Make a seamless transition from one training activity to the next activity.** Create transition statements to help learners see the connection between activities, as well as how each module relates to the next, so the training does not feel segmented. One example may be, "Filtering is one step in the process we can use to manage our time effectively. Let's take a look at another. . . ." The relationships between segments may be obvious to the training designer, but meaningful transition statements will help point out these connections to the participants.

◆ **Allow plenty of time for activity debriefings.** The debriefing discussions after each activity are crucial for the participants to commit to change their behavior and apply what they have learned. They also help clarify information and are an engaging way to determine whether the activity has been effective.

◆ **Create a detailed action plan for each session.** The samples in this workbook provide models for you to consider. Sometimes the training design includes activities for the facilitator and participants to do after the formal session.

◆ **Share the desired results for the training with the participants.** Present an overview of the desired outcomes for the training. Refer to them throughout the session as you transition between segments and activities, so learners see how the pieces fit together. This should be limited to three outcomes to be most effective.

◆ **Consider offering a follow-up session for participants.** Depending on the participants' and client organization's commitment and needs, plan a refresher session about a month or two after the training. During this meeting, you can facilitate a discussion of what worked well for the participants, what is still challenging for them, and what additional training sessions they would like to attend.

Tips on Designing Effective Training

When designing a training session, developers use a structured process to guide them and to ensure that the training is effective. This work is both an art and a science and reflects the designer's approach to adult learning.

A common process used for training design is represented by the acronym ADDIE, which represents each of the five steps in the process: analysis, design, development, implementation, and evaluation. Here is an explanation of this method:

- ◆ **Analysis.** Conduct a thorough needs assessment of the client organization and its learners (see chapter 2) to determine what the training issues are and what the desired results of the learning should be.

- ◆ **Design.** Decide how to present the training content to address the learners' needs according to your needs-assessment results and adult learning principles. Determine the sequencing of the training segments and structured activities during this step.

- ◆ **Development.** Create training materials such as PowerPoint presentations, handouts, participant manuals, and instructions for activities. This workbook provides the materials you will need to conduct effective time management training sessions, so you may not need to spend much time on this step.

- ◆ **Implementation.** Schedule the training session and handle any logistical details to conduct the training (book the facility, arrange catering, and make sure the materials and any necessary equipment are at the session). The facilitator must also market the training to potential participants and make any necessary changes to the content and materials.

- ◆ **Evaluation.** Assess whether the training has achieved the desired results and met the learners' needs. The different levels of evaluation are explained in more detail in chapter 5.

Because people usually remember the first and last things you say and do, it is important to pay attention to the beginning and ending activities when you design training. It is true that first impressions are critical for success and it can be difficult to recover from a poor start, so be sure to set yourself up for success. A strong ending will leave the participants feeling confident, informed, and excited to put into practice what they have learned. Your closing should emphasize a plan of action.

It's also a good idea to anticipate various problems that may occur, such as fire alarm interruptions, power outages, equipment failures, and domineering or difficult participants. A backup plan will help the training session go smoothly and will minimize stress for the facilitator.

It may also be beneficial to solicit feedback about your training design from colleagues beforehand to gauge the flow of the session and the appropriateness of activities. Ask one or more observers to sit in on a training session to help provide information on what may need to be changed and how the training can be most effective.

Ultimately, the training should be beneficial for the participants, the client organization, and the facilitator. To achieve this, the facilitator must have solid information about learning needs and also use resources carefully and to the fullest extent possible.

What to Do Next

- ◆ Determine how you will incorporate the principles of adult learning into your training sessions.

- ◆ Follow the suggestions for using the sample designs in this book, as outlined in this chapter.

- ◆ Use the ADDIE model for instructional design to help you select training content in line with your needs assessment data, and develop an effective workshop.

- ◆ Solicit feedback from others about your training design and planned workshop activities.

◆

Facilitating Time Management Training

What's in This Chapter?

- A definition of the facilitator role

- Strategies for engaging adult learners

- Techniques for capturing and holding trainees' attention

- Tips on creating a learning environment

The Role of the Facilitator

Facilitating training effectively combines the roles of event planner, public speaker, counselor, and entertainer.

- **Event planner.** The effective delivery of a training program requires effective coordination regarding facilities, equipment, materials, and participants. Contingency arrangements must be made for times when things don't go according to plan. Large training departments may provide administrative help with logistics planning, but when participants arrive, it's up to the facilitator to make sure everything is running smoothly. In larger groups, facilitation also involves crowd control. A big part of creating a productive learning environment includes making sure that the participants are back from breaks on time and are refocused.

- **Public speaker.** When you are the facilitator, the spotlight is on you. The participants look to you for behavioral cues, and your physical presence and speaking style set the tone for the program. You need to know your material so you can convey it to others. Because anything can happen in interactive design, you must also be able to think and react quickly.

◆ **Counselor.** A facilitator's most important skill is the ability to focus on the participants' verbal comments and physical cues and to understand their concerns and questions. It can be mentally exhausting to listen intently for an extended period of time, so be well rested and well prepared. This emphasis on the listening role is perhaps the most critical difference between a facilitator and the teachers most of us experienced as students.

◆ **Entertainer.** Few of us are good stand-up comedians (and we shouldn't try to be); nevertheless, participants feed on the energy of the facilitator. A low-energy, soft-spoken, unanimated facilitator will create a low-energy program with little interaction by participants. An engaging facilitator uses humor, interesting personal stories, sincere interest in the participants and subject matter, and—most important—high energy.

Although planning, effective speaking, listening, and demonstrating high energy increase the effectiveness of a facilitator, it is also important to be yourself. Emphasize your strengths and downplay skills or behaviors with which you are less comfortable. Don't try to be someone you're not. Use the materials in this book to design a training program well suited to your skills and personality.

What Is a Facilitator?

There can be confusion within the training and development field about the terminology used to denote persons or roles. Here are some useful distinctions:

◆ **Facilitator.** From the French word "facile," which means "easy," facilitation is the art and science of assisting learners in experiencing content. Because it is the subject of this chapter, the facilitator's role will soon become clearer—he or she "facilitates" learning for the group. Facilitation typically occurs in organizational meetings and training sessions.

◆ **Educator.** This is a person who teaches, or disseminates knowledge and understanding to students or pupils. The educator, or teacher, operates in classroom and laboratory settings, leading students from a position of authority and superior knowledge. In training and development terms, many educators play the role of subject matter expert.

◆ **Trainer.** This role centers on helping trainees become competent in the areas in which they are working. The focal points are specific job-task knowledge, skills, and effective practices. Trainers typically operate in training rooms with groups of trainees.

- ◆ **Counselor.** In an official capacity, requiring specialized education and training, a counselor provides private, confidential assistance to employees with personal problems. Not all training and development practitioners are qualified to serve in this role.

- ◆ **Consultant.** With special emphasis on working with employees in a partnership arrangement, consultants help clients analyze situations that need attention, explore and evaluate options, and commit to action plans. There are two basic types of consultants: expert and process. Experts give clients advice; process-oriented consultants help clients learn how to improve work processes, including interpersonal ones.

The facilitator, then, works with learners in a manner that helps them open themselves to new learning and makes the process easy. The role requires the facilitator not to be a subject matter expert, but instead, to set up activities that foster learning through hands-on experience and interaction. A common phrase used to define the facilitator's role is "to be the guide on the side and not the sage on the stage." Major aspects of excellence in facilitation include setting up proper experiential (participative) learning activities or exercises, as well as leading discussions of the results, referred to as debriefing. The structured experiences in chapter 12 include instructions to facilitate debriefings. It's important to spend at least as much time debriefing the exercises as conducting them, so participants understand how they will apply the training content to their real-life experiences.

Engaging Adult Learners

When thinking about principles of adult learning (see chapter 3), include a variety of activities in effective time management training that will engage the learners and encourage their participation. Although it is often necessary to convey information through lecture, for example, by going through Power-Point slides, a facilitator should spend no more than 15–20 minutes at a time on this type of presentation. The remainder of the time in each training module should focus on leading discussions, facilitating exercises, and otherwise engaging learners to make them active participants in the session.

Mixing the training methods used in a workshop provides variety for the facilitator and the learners; at the same time, it creates excellent opportunities for trainees to share their experiences, crystallize key concepts, and develop a plan of action for how they will apply the content of the training in their

everyday lives. Here are some common training methods that lead to participative learning:

- ◆ **Large-group discussions.** The facilitator poses questions to the full
  group of trainees; individual learners then respond to the questions
  in front of everyone, and others have the opportunity to add their
  ideas to the discussion. Each debriefing portion of the structured experiences in chapter 12 is meant to be a large-group discussion.

- ◆ **Small-group exercises.** Participants are divided into small groups
  (either by forming their own groups, numbering off, or a method
  chosen by the facilitator) in which they can have a discussion, hands-
  on activity, brainstorming, or problem-solving experience. Small
  groups usually have a time limit in which to complete their assignment, and one or more members of each group reports to the full
  group of trainees on what the group talked about, created, or decided.

- ◆ **Case studies.** Here, learners are provided with detailed information
  about a real-life situation, including all circumstances, issues, and actions of people related to the case study. Participants, working either
  individually or in small groups, must analyze the case study, discuss
  and share what was done well, what mistakes may have been made,
  and the implications of the case study for the topic at hand.

- ◆ **Role-plays.** Some adult learners may hear the words "role play" and
  want to run for the nearest exit. Role playing, however, is a very
  effective way for participants to practice new skills, particularly for
  interpersonal communication, in a safe environment. Two or more
  trainees spontaneously dramatize a situation that relates to a problem. Each participant acts out a role as he or she feels it would be
  portrayed in real life. After the other learners observe the performance, a debriefing discussion is usually held to talk about the role
  play and its implications. Although some role plays are conducted in
  front of the large group, and others are done in small groups, everyone watches the debriefing portion. The facilitator needs to be sensitive to the different learners' personalities when conducting a large-
  group role play, because some may be uncomfortable performing in
  front of more than a handful of people.

- ◆ **Simulations.** A simulation is an abstract representation of a real-
  life situation that requires learners to solve complex problems. The

facilitator creates aspects of the situation that are close to reality, and the learner must perform manipulations, respond, and take action to correct problems or maintain a certain status. Many simulations are computer controlled—for example, a flight simulator for airplane pilot training. After the training, the facilitator debriefs the learners and evaluates the results of the simulation.

◆ **Games.** A game is a formalized simulation activity. Two or more participants or teams compete with each other to meet a set of objectives relating to a training topic. Set rules and procedures for the game include information that requires decision-making and follow-up actions. Typically, the facilitator handles the scoring and may give small trinkets as prizes to the winning participants or teams. Games can be played in small or large groups.

To engage adult learners and ensure that learning is participative, it is important to use a variety of training methods. Equally important, the facilitator should capture and hold the participants' attention. Part of the facilitator's role is to guard against boredom; here are some techniques for keeping the learners interested:

◆ Open with an introductory exercise that captures learners' attention and gets them engaged within the first 15 minutes of the training session. This helps set the tone and communicates to the group that you value and encourage their participation.

◆ Vary your rate of speech, volume, movement, facial expressions, and gestures. Although it is best to maintain a good volume to be easily heard and avoid distracting gestures and mannerisms, these subtle techniques can emphasize what learners should attend to during the training.

◆ Break up explanations of key concepts with use of videos, demonstrations, examples, or readings from articles or books. This helps create memorable experiences for the participants and keeps things lively and interesting.

◆ Use appropriate and relevant humor, shock, suspense, or surprise. Share something unexpected, a funny anecdote, a startling statistic, or an applicable comic strip to engage learners and encourage discussion. These techniques provide good opportunities for trainees to identify with the content and explore different ideas.

Use Table 4–1 as a guide to help you decide which training methods to use and how you will engage learners so that their training experience is as participatory and effective as possible.

Table 4–1
Selecting Instructional Methods and Tools

Choosing Training Methods

For each module, determine which of the following instructional methods you will use
- ❏ Large-group discussions
- ❏ Small-group exercises
- ❏ Case studies
- ❏ Role plays
- ❏ Simulations
- ❏ Games
- ❏ Lectures.

Checking Training Design

For each module, make sure that you
- ❏ Identify the learning objectives
- ❏ Anticipate questions the participants may ask and formulate responses
- ❏ Include enough exercises for learners to demonstrate knowledge and share past experiences
- ❏ Provide correct responses (if applicable) and anticipate errors for each activity
- ❏ Include activities that enable learners to share how they will apply content to their work
- ❏ Allow sufficient time for debriefing discussions after exercises.

Logistics and Equipment

Check to be sure you have
- ❏ Secured and tested necessary equipment to conduct the training
- ❏ Produced ample copies of participant materials, assessments, and tools
- ❏ Saved a back-up copy of your PowerPoint presentation
- ❏ Secured (if applicable) and visited the training facility to assess the environment.

Table 4–1, continued

Selecting Instructional Methods and Tools

Other Issues to Consider

Have you provided an introductory activity that captures the attention of the learners within the first 15 minutes of the training?

❑ Yes   ❑ No

Do you have a plan for minimizing distractions during the training and communicating this to the participants?

❑ Yes   ❑ No

Have you practiced presenting the PowerPoint slides and conducting the activities in your training session?

❑ Yes   ❑ No

Do you have a plan for varying your actions and creating memorable experiences for the learners during the training?

❑ Yes   ❑ No

Adapted from: Carliner, Saul. *Training Design Basics.* Alexandria, Virginia: ASTD, 2003.

Creating the Learning Environment

Creating a positive learning environment is a critical factor in making learning easy. The facilitator should seek to create four conditions to maximize learning:

- ◆ **Confidentiality.** The first step to learning is to admit ignorance. Some trainees may fear the repercussions of showing their weaknesses. To alleviate these concerns, assure participants that the sole purpose of the training is to build their time management and organization skills, and that no evaluations will take place. If discussions and events during the training program remain confidential between the participants and the facilitator, this will help create a safe, risk-free environment.

- ◆ **Freedom from distractions.** Work and personal demands cannot be ignored during training, but they should be minimized as a courtesy to others; this will help each participant benefit from the training to the fullest extent possible. Ask that cell phones, personal digital assistants, and pagers be turned off or set to inaudible alerts. Selecting a training site away from the workplace will help to reduce distractions greatly. Acknowledge that although participants don't have time to be away from work, they should immerse themselves in the learning experience to benefit fully from their time in training. You can also remind them that they will have plenty of opportunities to check messages during breaks.

◆ **Participants are responsible for their own learning.** Experiential (participatory) learning requires that trainees be actively engaged and committed to learning. The facilitator can only create the opportunity to learn; he or she cannot force anyone to learn. If a participant leaves a well-designed training session (which use of this book guarantees!) saying, "I learned nothing," then that statement reflects on the participant more than on the facilitator. The facilitator's role is to create a learning environment in which participants are challenged, intrigued, and able to explore and address their own developmental needs. It's the participants' responsibility to respond to the learning environment and, if necessary, to inform the facilitator if the environment is not meeting their needs.

◆ **All participants are learning partners.** Each participant brings some relevant knowledge to the training program. In a successful training session, each participant should share information through discussion. Encourage all participants to accept responsibility for helping others learn.

 ## What to Do Next

◆ **Plan.** Make sure you are prepared to use all of the elements of your design effectively. Ensure that your facilitation style is as appropriate as possible. What will you be working on? What skills do you want to sharpen while facilitating this training? How will you obtain coaching and feedback on these skills?

◆ **Practice.** Go through the training materials in your design carefully. Be prepared to respond to any questions that the trainees might have about the materials and activities. Present the PowerPoint slide shows to a friend or colleague to become more comfortable with the points you want to make.

◆ **Recruit co-facilitators.** You and your trainees can benefit from having co-facilitators, but it can be confusing and excessive to have more than two at once. The active involvement of an experienced manager or executive as a co-facilitator can be a wonderful addition; however, you may need to coach the person to play the role of trainer. Subject matter experts, such as a well-known motivator or teacher, can also add depth and credibility. You will need to coach each of the subject matter experts before and after the session for maximum effectiveness and minimal surprises.

◆ **Prepare all needed materials and test your equipment.** Using the website that accompanies this book, print enough copies of the assessments and training instruments needed in your design. Set up your computer to project the PowerPoint slide shows, and rehearse the ones called for by your design.

◆

Evaluating and Improving Time Management Training

What's in This Chapter?

- ◆ Overview of a classic training evaluation model
- ◆ How to use included instruments for your own training evaluation
- ◆ Tips on interpreting and making use of evaluation results
- ◆ Steps to successful evaluation

Why Bother?

Evaluating training can be extremely beneficial to both the trainer and the organization. Without an evaluation, you are essentially flying blind; you don't know whether the training is effective, whether participants learn anything during the training, or whether it has a positive impact on the organization.

Here are three motivations for, and benefits of, evaluating the time management training you design and deliver:

1. The training outcomes need to be aligned with the learning needs that you assessed earlier. In other words, did the training meet the needs the learners in the organization had at the time?

2. You can justify the continuation of investing in time management and other training you provide if you can demonstrate that it is on target.

   - ◆ Did the learners like the training?
   - ◆ Did they learn the content?
   - ◆ Did they use the content?
   - ◆ Did it positively affect the organization's results?

3. By using a scientific approach to improve the design and delivery of the training you provide, you can demonstrate value to the organization by linking data to business decisions. Thoroughly evaluating time management training ensures that the continuous improvement of your training is driven by real information and not just by general impressions or anecdotes. It also conveys the message that you are serious about results, and it demonstrates your business acumen.

The Classic Levels of Training Evaluation

Donald Kirkpatrick (2006) developed a well-known model for training evaluation that consists of four levels and guides much of the practice of measuring training outcomes in the learning and development field. The levels are graduated, from the relatively easy to measure to the more complex.

Level 1—Reaction: Measuring the reaction of participants to the training. Although positive reactions may not ensure that learning takes place, negative reactions can certainly affect the likelihood of learning and whether the training will be offered again in the future.

Level 2—Learning: Measuring the extent to which learning objectives have been achieved. Has knowledge increased? Have skills improved or attitudes changed as a result of the training?

Level 3—Behavior: Measuring the extent to which participants changed their behavior in the organization because they attended the training.

Level 4—Results: Measuring the organizational results from behavioral changes that were achieved because participants attended the training.

The least powerful, but most common, evaluation method is at the first level; they are brief reaction surveys commonly called "Smile Sheets" which usually use Likert scales to answer questions regarding the effectiveness of the training content and delivery, and often include space to write comments. These questions are often asked in terms of value and participant enjoyment of the training.

Smile Sheets indicate immediate reactions of participants, but they may have no correlation to actual learning. An entertaining facilitator, comfortable learning environment, and good food can produce positive survey results, but they may not affect application of learning and behavior change. Also, some participants follow the old adage, "If you can't say anything nice, don't say anything at all." They may either give high scores that don't reflect their real reactions, or they may not complete the evaluation. They may also be more concerned with leaving the training facility and beating rush hour traffic than providing helpful feedback.

Organizations often use Smile Sheets because they are easy to administer and can provide some value. Positive scores may not be indicative of effective training, but negative evaluations are a strong indication that the training is ineffective. Open-ended questions that allow participants to provide comments on the training can also offer important, useful feedback.

Because the four evaluation levels are ranked according to complexity, they are also, in effect, ranked according to decreasing use. More organizations therefore use only Smile Sheets to evaluate training rather than attempt to measure learning and impact at the other three levels. Some may track learning by conducting pretests and posttests to assess skill level, but this may be limited to information technology training subjects in many organizations. Fewer track behavior change, and still fewer engage in the difficult task of measuring business results or return-on-investment for learning programs. The author strongly recommends that trainers take whatever steps they need to evaluate their sessions more thoroughly. If training is to be thought of as a key business activity, trainers need to be accountable for the value they claim to add to the organization and the impact on results.

Instruments for Evaluation in This Workbook

Chapter 11 of this workbook includes four instruments that lend themselves to applications of evaluating training. Some can also be used in training designs.

◆ **Assessment 11–2: Time Management Self-Assessment.** This tool calls for time management training participants to analyze their strengths and developmental needs. The instrument can be used not only as prework for an initial training module, but also as a repeat measure either at the end of the session or some time afterward.

◆ **Assessment 11–4: Facilitator Competencies.** This form helps establish learning priorities for your own development as a workshop facilitator. It can be used as a self-assessment or as a follow-up questionnaire to solicit feedback from trainees after a session or at a later time.

◆ **Assessment 11–5: Time Management Skills Follow-Up Assessment.** Distribute this questionnaire some time after the time management training. It targets Level 3 of Kirkpatrick's training evaluation model, and it can be used in follow-up reunions of trainees or as a survey. The questionnaire can also include ratings from colleagues or supervisors in the participants' work environments.

◆ **Assessment 11–6: Training Evaluation.** Use this form to conduct a Level 1 Smile Sheet evaluation. It allows training participants to provide reaction feedback about the workshop and the facilitator.

Of course, trainers are not limited to using these four instruments. It is important to commit yourself to systematic evaluation and to conduct it routinely. In this way, you build up an understanding of what works best with your trainees and communicate your value to the client organization.

Improving Time Management Training

For many organizations, the concept of continuous improvement is of critical importance. As a training professional, it is in your best interest to demonstrate your attention to detail, as well as how you achieve the desired results. Be proactive to set yourself up for success; this will enable you to meet the needs of the organization and of its learners in the best way possible. Applied to time management training, commitment to continuous improvement means

◆ Specifying the steps you are taking

◆ Analyzing the logic of the sequence

◆ Looking carefully at the effectiveness of each step

◆ Making changes that offer chances to make the training better.

This approach requires documentation and careful evaluation of the effects, or outcomes, of each step.

Pay close attention to clients' needs to provide work of high quality to organizations. In training, this means assessing the learning needs and preferences of potential participants; involving them in evaluating the training; and providing other services, such as one-on-one coaching, to them as they apply what they learn to their everyday work.

Trainers should avoid using their favorite learning activities; they should be more flexible and adapt to different organization and learner needs. A better approach to improving training is to experiment with both the content and design of the session. If activities do not produce desired results, either change or discontinue them. Try new ways and new activities to deliver the same learning objectives.

Learn ways to evaluate training on more than one of Kirkpatrick's levels. This may include activities such as investigating how pretests and posttests can enhance learning application in a Level 2 evaluation; researching and implementing behavior assessments or interviewing learners' colleagues and supervisors to get Level 3 data; or working to understand and use performance measures before and after training, such as productivity statistics or sales figures, to conduct a Level 4 evaluation. The data gleaned through using Levels 2 through 4 of the model can provide great insight into how to improve your time management training. This is more time consuming than simply distributing a Smile Sheet, but the payoff can be substantial. Please see the For Further Reading resource at the back of this book for additional resources on training measurement and evaluation.

When time has passed after your training, you can also solicit feedback on your competence as a trainer and facilitator. This information can guide you through the process of developing as a learning professional. The root cause of less-than-optimal time management training is often the trainer, not the design. You may be interfering with the effectiveness of your sessions. Asking for feedback on what you can change is a direct way to manage your growth as a trainer, but soliciting honest feedback may not be a natural, comfortable thing for some people to do. You can become a role model for other trainers by actively engaging learners in your own quest for excellence.

What to Do Next

Here is a step-by-step method to maximize the benefits of evaluating your time management training sessions:

- ◆ **Decide which steps to follow.** Lay out a step-by-step plan to evaluate the outcomes (impacts and payoffs) of your time management training. Be specific about your goals (who will do what, when, how much, and for what purpose). Establish a timeline for these steps.

◆ **Gather feedback.** Solicit data from trainees and all relevant others. Use the instruments included in this book to assist you in this process.

◆ **Analyze results.** Conduct both statistical and content analyses of the responses you receive while gathering data for your evaluation. Be as objective as possible during this step because you may be predisposed to use the data to validate your own opinions and observations.

◆ **Modify the design as necessary.** Your evaluation program is the beginning of your design improvement process. Use the results to strengthen what works well, and change the selection, content, or sequence of activities to reach your training objectives more effectively.

◆

Individual/Small-Group Session

- ◆ Advice on working with individuals and small groups

- ◆ Considerations for choosing the right content for training sessions

- ◆ Step-by-step preparation and training delivery instructions

- ◆ Sample agendas

The materials in this workbook, which are designed to meet a variety of training needs, cover a range of topics related to time management trainees and can be offered in many formats and timeframes. Although lengthy immersion in the training environment can enhance learning experiences and increase their depth, sometimes training must be done in short, small doses. The size of the organization, as well as work demands, may also limit the number of participants available at any particular time. This chapter discusses session designs for time management trainees individually and in small groups.

Individual Session

TRAINING OBJECTIVES

The objectives of an individual training session are to convey as much information as possible to the participant in a short time, as well as to build the one-on-one relationship between the trainer and the participant. This interaction between the trainer and the participant is the greatest advantage of individual training sessions. The participant's specific questions and issues can be explored in greater depth than in a session with multiple participants.

An individual training session is appropriate in the following circumstances:

- ◆ The targeted, available audience for training is one person.

- ◆ One individual requires training in one particular content area.

- ◆ Training facilities for multiple participants are not available.

 ### *TIME*

- ◆ 1 hour to 2 hours, 45 minutes

CHOOSING THE CONTENT

One of the advantages of training a single participant is the ability to select content specifically for an individual's needs. Although all of the content modules in this book can be used for individual training, some are more easily tailored than others. The structured experiences in this book typically require multiple participants, but some exercises are appropriate for a single participant working with a trainer. The content modules most appropriate for an individual training session are:

- ◆ Content Module 10–2: Time Management Defined

- ◆ Content Module 10–3: Time Management Self-Assessment

- ◆ Content Module 10–4: The Time Management Process

- ◆ Content Module 10–5: Goal-Setting

- ◆ Content Module 10–6: Scheduling Time and Tasks

- ◆ Content Module 10–8: Procrastination

- ◆ Content Module 10–10: Managing Email

- ◆ Content Module 10–11: Working With Paperwork

These modules are in chapter 10.

Although all of the modules are not readily adaptable to individual training sessions, there is enough content suitable for one-on-one training to cover a wide range of time management issues. Your training needs assessment will help you set priorities and select the content modules of highest value for your audience.

The timing of certain topics is another thing to consider when choosing content. For instance, the "Time Management Defined" module introduces us to the concept of time management and provides a foundation for the other modules. It should be offered first if a series of modules will be presented. The "Time Management Self-Assessment" module helps to focus the learning efforts of the trainee and should be offered early in the training process. "The Time Management Process," "Goal-Setting," and "Scheduling Time and Tasks" modules help the learner understand ways to set priorities when planning use of time, and provide the learner with a specific process to manage time effectively. These are ideally offered before the "Procrastination," "Managing Email," and "Working With Paperwork" modules.

The sample agenda is designed for someone who is beginning his or her training on time management. It contains the "Time Management Defined" and "Time Management Self-Assessment" modules.

MATERIALS

For the instructor:

- This chapter for reference

- Content Module 10–2: Time Management Defined

- Content Module 10–3: Time Management Self-Assessment

- Structured Experience 12–1: Time Management Buddies (with trainer acting as participant's partner)

- Structured Experience 12–2: A Waste of Time (with trainer brainstorming with the participant)

- PowerPoint presentation: Time Management Defined. To access slides for this program, open the file *Time Management Defined.ppt* on the accompanying website. Copies of the slides for this training session are included at the end of chapter 9 (slides 9–1 through 9–10).

For the participant:

- Assessment 11–2: Time Management Self-Assessment

- Writing instruments

- Blank paper for taking notes

SAMPLE AGENDA

8:00 a.m.	Introductions (5 minutes)
8:05	Content Module 10–2: Time Management Defined (chapter 10) (1 hour, 30 minutes)
9:35	Break (10 minutes)
9:45	Content Module 10–3: Time Management Self-Assessment (chapter 10) (1 hour)
10:45	Close

STEP-BY-STEP PLANNING

At the training session:

- Introduce yourself to the participant. Include a description of your role in the training process, as well as your training and work experience. First impressions count, and this is your chance to establish credibility with the participant.

- Ask the participant to introduce himself or herself to you, including his or her name, role, and what he or she would like to gain from the training. Let the participant know that this is an informal session, and try to put him or her at ease.

- Review the agenda and learning objectives with the participant.

- Go through the selected content module(s).

- Take a break about an hour to an hour and a half after the session has begun.

- Ask for questions and test for understanding frequently.

- Close the session with an opportunity for the participant to ask questions. If appropriate, offer your help and availability on an ongoing basis.

Small-Group Session

TRAINING OBJECTIVES

The objectives of a small-group training session are to convey as much information as possible to the participants in a short period of time, and to build relationships between the trainer and the participants. The small-group setting allows in-depth discussion of a limited set of issues.

A small-group training session is appropriate for the following circumstances:

- The targeted training audience consists of seven people or fewer.

- A few individuals require training in one particular content area.

- Training facilities for large groups are not available.

TIME

- 1 hour to 2 hours, 15 minutes

CHOOSING THE CONTENT

Any of the content modules in this book can be used for small-group training. Select the module(s) based on the needs assessment of the particular group.

This sample agenda assumes that the most pressing need for this small group is to have a model they can use to improve their time management skills. We've selected the "Participant Introductions" and "The Time Management Process" modules. The former module is an introduction exercise that helps create the learning environment by preparing the participants to act as learning partners and share common features of their time management skills. The latter module enables participants to use a process with specific steps to help them manage time more effectively, and it provides them with an opportunity to explore their roles and responsibilities, as well as to analyze where their time is spent.

MATERIALS

For the instructor:

- This chapter for reference

- Content Module 10–1: Participant Introductions

- Content Module 10–4: The Time Management Process

- Structured Experience 12–3: Roles and Responsibilities

- Structured Experience 12–4: Where Does the Time Go?

◆ PowerPoint presentation: The Time Management Process. To access slides for this program, open the file *The Time Management Process.ppt* on the accompanying website. Copies of the slides for this training session are included at the end of chapter 9 (slides 9–11 through 9–28).

For the participants:

◆ Writing instruments and blank paper

◆ Participants' printouts of last week's calendar and task list, pages from a planner, or information on a personal digital assistant.

SAMPLE AGENDA

8:00 a.m.   Content Module 10–1: Participant Introductions (chapter 10) (15 minutes)

8:15   Content Module 10–4: The Time Management Process (chapter 10) (2 hours)

10:15   Close

STEP-BY-STEP PLANNING

Just before the training session:

◆ Arrive early at the facility.

◆ Set up and test equipment (for example, laptop, projector, and flipcharts).

At the training session:

◆ Introduce yourself to the participants. Include a description of your role in the training process, as well as your training and work experience. First impressions count, and this is your chance to establish credibility with the participants.

◆ If you do not use the participant introductions exercise, ask the participants to introduce themselves by sharing their names, roles, and what they would like to gain from the training. Let them know they will be helping each other learn.

◆ Review the agenda and learning objectives with the participants.

◆ Go through the selected content module(s).

◆ Take a break about an hour after the session has begun.

◆ Ask for questions and test for understanding frequently.

◆ Close the session with an opportunity for the participants to ask questions. If appropriate, offer your help and availability on an ongoing basis.

What to Do Next

◆ Identify the training participant(s) and assess their most critical training needs.

◆ Determine the time available for the training session.

◆ Select the highest value content module(s) based on needs and time available.

◆ Schedule the session.

◆ Arrange a facility for the training session.

◆ Invite the participant(s).

◆ Send a confirmation to participants. Include an agenda and any advance work with the confirmation.

◆ Prepare training materials (for example, handouts, overheads, and presentations).

◆

Half-Day Session

What's in This Chapter?

- ◆ Advice on choosing the content for training sessions

- ◆ Step-by-step preparation and training delivery instructions

- ◆ Sample agendas

The materials in this workbook can be used for a variety of training needs and timeframes, and this chapter covers designs suitable for half-day (four-hour) training sessions. Because contributions from a variety of participants enhance the learning environment, group training is generally more effective and enjoyable than one-on-one training sessions and should be used whenever possible. Group learning dynamics can be obtained with only three participants, but a group of between 12 and 24 participants is best.

Objectives and Use

The objectives of a half-day training session are to build understanding of the learning content that is of greatest value to the organization and the participants, as well as to build relationships between the trainer and the participants. The group setting allows for rich and diverse discussion of the various topics.

A half-day training session is appropriate for the following circumstances:

- ◆ The targeted, available audience for training is three or more.

- ◆ The targeted audience requires training in several content areas.

- ◆ Training facilities for groups are available.

- ◆ The time available for the training session is limited to four hours.

Choosing the Content

Any of the content modules in this book can be used for half-day training sessions. Select the modules based on the needs assessment of the participant group. If the participant group does not have an identified set of assessed needs (for example, if an assessment was not completed or an open registration process is being used), select the modules based on the competencies the organization seeks to develop.

Consider the order of certain topics when selecting which content will be offered first. As noted in the previous chapter, use the "Time Management Defined" and "Time Management Self-Assessment" modules early in the training process. The sample designs in this chapter include these modules in the first of several half-day sessions that together cover all of the book's content modules.

Note: When your training session is at least a half day long, you've crossed the refreshment threshold. Hunger and thirst are enemies to the learning environment, so offer beverages and snacks at the breaks so your participants' biological needs are met.

For the first sample agenda, we've selected the "Participant Introductions," "Time Management Defined," and "Time Management Self-Assessment" modules.

Sample Agenda One

The "Participant Introductions" module is an introduction exercise that helps create the learning environment by preparing the participants to act as learning partners and share common characteristics of their time management skills. The "Time Management Defined" module introduces us to the concept of time management and sets the foundation for the rest of the time management training. The "Time Management Self-Assessment" module helps participants recognize learning opportunities that offer the greatest leverage for improving their time management skills.

 TIME

- ◆ 3 hours, 15 minutes

MATERIALS

For the instructor:

- ◆ Content module 10–1: Participant Introductions

- ◆ Content Module 10–2: Time Management Defined

- ◆ Content Module 10–3: Time Management Self-Assessment

- ◆ Structured Experience 12–1: Time Management Buddies

- ◆ Structured Experience 12–2: A Waste of Time

- ◆ PowerPoint presentation: Time Management Defined. To access slides for this program, open the file *Time Management Defined.ppt* on the accompanying website. Copies of the slides for this training session are included at the end of chapter 9 (slides 9–1 through 9–10).

For the participants:

- ◆ Assessment 11–2: Time Management Self-Assessment

- ◆ Writing instruments

- ◆ Blank paper for taking notes

SAMPLE AGENDA

8:00 a.m. Content Module 10–1: Participant Introductions (chapter 10) (30 minutes; varies by class size)

Objective: Prepare participants to help each other learn.

8:30 Content Module 10–2: Time Management Defined (chapter 10) (1 hour, 30 minutes)

Objective: Understand what time management is and the importance of recognizing behaviors that waste time.

10:00 Break (10 minutes)

10:10 Content Module 10–3: Time Management Self-Assessment (chapter 10) (1 hour)

Objective: Identify each participant's highest-impact learning opportunities.

11:10   Close (5 minutes)

              Objective: Reinforce learning points.

11:15   Participants dismissed.

Sample Agenda Two

Including breaks, this design falls just under the four-hour mark. "The Time Management Process" module helps participants use a process with specific steps to help them manage time more effectively. It also provides them with an opportunity to analyze the roles and responsibilities they have, and to look at how they spend their time. The "Goal-Setting" module looks at the importance of having specific, achievable goals in good time management and includes detailed steps for goal achievement, along with a planning tool.

TIME

- ◆ 3 hours, 50 minutes

MATERIALS

For the instructor:

- ◆ Content Module 10–4: The Time Management Process

- ◆ Content Module 10–5: Goal-Setting

- ◆ Structured Experience 12–3: Roles and Responsibilities

- ◆ Structured Experience 12–4: Where Does the Time Go?

- ◆ Structured Experience 12–5: Goal-Setting Practice

- ◆ PowerPoint presentation: The Time Management Process. To access slides for this program, open the file *The Time Management Process.ppt* on the accompanying website. Copies of the slides for this training session are included at the end of chapter 9 (slides 9–11 through 9–28).

- ◆ PowerPoint presentation: Goal-Setting. To access slides for this program, open the file *Goal-Setting.ppt* on the accompanying website. Copies of the slides for this training session are included at the end of chapter 9 (slides 9–29 through 9–38).

For the participants:

- ◆ Training Instrument 11–1: Goal-Setting Worksheet

- ◆ Writing instruments and blank paper

- ◆ Participants' printouts of last week's calendar and task list, pages from a planner, or information on a personal digital assistant.

SAMPLE AGENDA

8:00 a.m. Content Module 10–4: The Time Management Process (chapter 10) (2 hours)

Objective: Understand a process to use for time management with specific steps for greater effectiveness.

10:00 Break (15 minutes)

10:15 Content Module 10–5: Goal-Setting (chapter 10) (1 hour, 30 minutes)

Objective: Understand the importance of setting goals in relation to time management, and steps to take for goal achievement.

11:45 Close (5 minutes)

Objective: Reinforce learning points.

11:50 Participants dismissed.

Sample Agenda Three

This agenda covers the "Time Management Defined," "Scheduling Time and Tasks," and "Effective Delegation" modules. The "Time Management Defined" module provides an introduction to the concept of time management and sets the foundation for the rest of the time management training. The "Scheduling Time and Tasks" module gives participants the opportunity to practice planning their time and introduces a helpful tool for this purpose. The "Effective Delegation" module looks at current delegating behavior and provides tips for improving delegation to ease stress and increase focus.

TIME

- ◆ 4 hours, 15 minutes

MATERIALS

For the instructor:

- ◆ Content Module 10–2: Time Management Defined

- ◆ Content Module 10–6: Scheduling Time and Tasks

- ◆ Content Module 10–7: Effective Delegation

- ◆ Structured Experience 12–1: Time Management Buddies

- ◆ Structured Experience 12–2: A Waste of Time

- ◆ Structured Experience 12–6: Getting Around to It

- ◆ Structured Experience 12–7: Delightful Delegating

- ◆ PowerPoint presentation: Time Management Defined Process. To access slides for this program, open the file Time Management *Defined.ppt* on the accompanying website. Copies of the slides for this training session are included at the end of chapter 9 (slides 9–1 through 9–10).

- ◆ PowerPoint presentation: Scheduling Time and Tasks. To access slides for this program, open the file *Scheduling Time and Tasks.ppt* on the accompanying website. Copies of the slides for this training session are included at the end of chapter 9 (slides 9–39 through 9–46).

- ◆ PowerPoint presentation: Effective Delegation. To access slides for this program, open the file *Effective Delegation.ppt* on the accompanying website. Copies of the slides for this training session are included at the end of chapter 9 (slides 9–47 through 9–53).

For the participants:

- ◆ Training Instrument 11–2: Scheduling Sheet

- ◆ Participants' current schedule of upcoming tasks and appointments or sample tasks and appointments (optional)

- ◆ Writing instruments and blank paper

SAMPLE AGENDA

8:00 a.m. Content Module 10–2: Time Management Defined (chapter 10) (1 hour, 30 minutes)

Objective: Understand what time management is and the importance of recognizing behaviors that waste time.

9:30 Content Module 10–6: Scheduling Time and Tasks (chapter 10) (1 hour, 15 minutes)

Objective: Learn steps and techniques for scheduling time, and gain practice using a planning tool.

10:45 Break (10 minutes)

10:55 Content Module 10-7: Effective Delegation (chapter 10) (1 hour, 15 minutes)

Objective: Identify current behaviors for delegating, and learn strategies to delegate more for lower stress and increased focus.

12:10 p.m. Close (5 minutes)

Objective: Reinforce learning points.

12:15 Participants dismissed.

Sample Agenda Four

This agenda contains two modules: "Procrastination" and "Interruptions and Distractions."

TIME

◆ 2 hours, 45 minutes

MATERIALS

For the instructor:

◆ Content Module 10–8: Procrastination

◆ Content Module 10–9: Interruptions and Distractions

◆ Structured Experience 12–8: Excuses, Excuses

◆ Structured Experience 12–9: Interruption Role-Play

◆ PowerPoint presentation: Procrastination. To access slides for this program, open the file *Procrastination.ppt* on the accompanying website. Copies of the slides for this training session are included at the end of chapter 9 (slides 9–54 through 9–60).

◆ PowerPoint presentation: Interruptions and Distractions. To access slides for this program, open the file *Interruptions and Distractions.ppt* on the accompanying website. Copies of the slides for this training session are included at the end of chapter 9 (slides 9–61 through 9–70).

For the participants:

◆ Assessment 11–7: Interruptions Self-Assessment

◆ Handout 12–1: Procrastinating Phrases

◆ Handout 12-2: Interruption Role-Play Scenarios

◆ Writing instruments

SAMPLE AGENDA

8:00 a.m.   Content Module 10–8: Procrastination (chapter 10) (1 hour)

Objective: Explore the many ways people procrastinate, and learn techniques to overcome procrastination.

9:00   Break (10 minutes)

9:10   Content Module 10–9: Interruptions and Distractions (chapter 10) (1 hour, 30 minutes)

Objective: Understand the common ways people interrupt others, and practice strategies for managing interruptions and distractions in the workplace.

10:40   Close (5 minutes)

Objective: Reinforce learning points.

10:45   Participants dismissed.

Sample Agenda Five

This agenda contains the remaining modules, "Managing Email" and "Working with Paperwork."

TIME

- 3 hours, 30 minutes

MATERIALS

For the instructor:

- Content Module 10–10: Managing Email

- Content Module 10–11: Working With Paperwork

- Structured Experience 12–10: Super Subject Lines

- Structured Experience 12–11: Problem Paper

- Structured Experience 12–12: Organization Action Plan

- PowerPoint presentation: Managing Email. To access slides for this program, open the file *Managing Email.ppt* on the accompanying website. Copies of the slides for this training session are included at the end of chapter 9 (slides 9–71 through 9–80).

- PowerPoint presentation: Working With Paperwork. To access slides for this program, open the file *Working With Paperwork.ppt* on the accompanying website. Copies of the slides for this training session are included at the end of chapter 9 (slides 9–81 through 9–92).

- Materials for small groups to sort provided by the facilitator (such as scribbled meeting notes, magazine articles, business memos, sample invoices, training handouts, party invitations, and sample reports)

- Blank slips of paper or sticky notes

For the participants:

- Training Instrument 11–3: Organization Action Plan

- Handout 12–3: Subject Line Practice

- Handout 12–4: Paperwork Samples

- Writing instruments

SAMPLE AGENDA

8:00 a.m.   Content Module 10–10: Managing Email (chapter 10) (1 hour, 15 minutes)

Objective: Learn techniques and etiquette for working with email that lead to better productivity and efficiency with less frustration.

9:15   Break (10 minutes)

9:25   Content Module 10–11: Working With Paperwork (chapter 10) (2 hours)

Objective: Understand and practice simple steps to deal with clutter, and effectively manage paper in the office.

11:25   Close (5 minutes)

Objective: Reinforce learning points.

11:30   Participants dismissed.

Step-by-Step Planning

Just before the training session:

- ◆ Arrive at the facility early.

- ◆ Set up and test equipment (laptop, projector, and flipcharts).

- ◆ Confirm refreshments.

At the training session:

- ◆ Introduce yourself to the participants. Include a description of your role in the training process, as well as your training and work experience. First impressions count, and this is your chance to establish credibility with the participants.

- ◆ If you do not use the participant introductions exercise, ask the participants to introduce themselves by sharing their names, roles, and what they would like to gain from the training. Let them know they will be helping each other learn.

- ◆ Review the agenda and learning objectives with the participants.

- ◆ Go through the selected content modules.

- ◆ Ask for questions and test for understanding frequently.

- ◆ Close the session with an opportunity for the participants to ask questions. If appropriate, offer your help and availability on an ongoing basis.

At the second through fifth sessions:

- ◆ Review the agenda and learning objectives with the participants.

- ◆ Go through the selected content modules.

- ◆ Ask for questions and test for understanding frequently.

- ◆ Close the session with an opportunity for the participants to ask questions. If appropriate, offer your help and availability on an on-going basis.

What to Do Next

- ◆ Identify the training participants and assess their most critical training needs, or identify the competencies the organization seeks to develop.

- ◆ Determine the agenda based on the highest value content modules called for by your needs assessment or the required competencies.

- ◆ Schedule the session.

- ◆ Arrange a facility for the training session.

- ◆ Invite participants.

- ◆ Send a confirmation to participants. Include an agenda and any pre-work with the confirmation.

- ◆ Prepare training materials (handouts, overheads, presentations, and exercise materials).

- ◆ Order food and beverages.

◆

Full-Day Session

- ◆ Advice on choosing the content for training sessions

- ◆ Step-by-step preparation and training delivery instructions

- ◆ Sample agendas

The materials in this workbook have been designed to meet a variety of training needs and timeframes, and this chapter covers designs suitable for full-day (six- to eight-hour) training sessions.

Full-day training sessions, and those that are even longer, might raise concerns that participants will be overloaded with information. Nevertheless, the benefits of extended learning experiences can outweigh the potential drawbacks. A shorter program might be seen as part of a typical workday, but a longer program can become a memorable life experience for the participant, particularly if it is held at an offsite venue. It often takes a different physical environment and a complete break from daily routine for participants to focus on learning. The learning environment discussed in chapter 4 is more readily established in extended programs in which the synergistic relationships of the various time management competencies can be more thoroughly explored. Full-day sessions are appropriate for group training. The backgrounds and experiences of a variety of participants enhance the learning environment. For full-day sessions, a group of between 12 and 24 participants is best.

Although this chapter includes illustrative designs, the trainer should adapt them to fit the training purposes. Each design can be modified to take into account the resources available; the learning readiness of potential participants; and, above all, the assessed development needs of the learners and the organization.

Objectives and Use

The objectives of a full-day training session are to free participants from their daily routine so they are open to develop an understanding of the learning content that is of greatest value, as well as to build relationships between the trainer and the participants. The group setting allows for rich and diverse discussion of the various topics.

A full-day training session is appropriate for the following circumstances:

- ◆ The targeted, available audience for training is 12 or more.

- ◆ The targeted audience requires training in several content areas.

- ◆ Training facilities for groups are available.

- ◆ A full day is available for the training session.

- ◆ Funding for meals (and optionally) for an offsite location is available.

Choosing the Content

Any of the content modules in this book can be used as part of a full-day training session. Select the modules based on the needs assessment of the participant group. If the participant group does not have an identified set of assessed needs (either an assessment was not completed, or an open registration process is being used), select the modules based on the competencies the organization seeks to develop.

As noted for half-day sessions, the entire curriculum contained in this book can also be offered in a series of full-day sessions.

When your training session is at least a full day long, you've crossed over the meal threshold. Hunger and thirst are enemies to the learning environment, so offer beverages and snacks at the breaks so your participants' biological needs are met. Lunch for participants is strongly suggested. Keep participants together during the lunch break to encourage continuing discussion of learning points. This also helps to strengthen the relationships between participants and, therefore, helps support the learning environment. In addition, a scheduled lunch discourages participants from going back to the office and getting distracted from their learning focus. Finally, providing lunch helps to keep your session on schedule because participants are less likely to come back late from the lunch break.

Three sample agendas are included. Each is designed as a stand-alone training session. Each agenda reflects a different major training issue pertaining to time management skills.

Sample Agenda One

This agenda reflects a requirement for training about basic time management skills and how participants can learn by following a specific process. This may have been identified as an organizational competency or as a common need for the participants. The timing of "The Time Management Process" module assumes that both structured experiences for the module are conducted and the exact allocation of time is up to the workshop facilitator.

TIME

- ◆ 7 hours, 15 minutes

MATERIALS

For the instructor:

- ◆ Content Module 10–1: Participant Introductions

- ◆ Content Module 10–2: Time Management Defined

- ◆ Content Module 10–4: The Time Management Process

- ◆ Content Module 10–5: Goal-Setting

- ◆ Structured Experience 12–1: Time Management Buddies

- ◆ Structured Experience 12–2: A Waste of Time

- ◆ Structured Experience 12–3: Roles and Responsibilities

- ◆ Structured Experience 12–4: Where Does the Time Go?

- ◆ Structured Experience 12–5: Goal-Setting Practice

- ◆ PowerPoint presentation: Time Management Defined. To access slides for this program, open the file *Time Management Defined.ppt* on the accompanying website. Copies of the slides for this training session are included at the end of chapter 9 (slides 9–1 through 9–10).

- PowerPoint presentation: The Time Management Process. To access slides for this program, open the file *Time Management Process.ppt* on the accompanying website. Copies of the slides for this training session are included at the end of chapter 9 (slides 9–11 through 9–28).

- PowerPoint presentation: Goal-Setting. To access slides for this program, open the file *Goal-Setting.ppt* on the accompanying website. Copies of the slides for this training session are included at the end of chapter 9 (slides 9–29 through 9–38).

For the participants:

- Training Instrument 11–1: Goal-Setting Worksheet

- Participants' printouts of last week's calendar and task list, pages from a planner, or information on a personal digital assistant.

- Writing instruments and blank paper

SAMPLE AGENDA

8:00 a.m. Content Module 10–1: Participant Introductions (chapter 10) (45 minutes; varies by class size)

Objective: Prepare participants to help each other learn.

8:45 Content Module 10–2: Time Management Defined (chapter 10) (1 hour, 30 minutes)

Objective: Understand what time management is and the importance of recognizing behaviors that waste time.

10:15 Break (15 minutes)

10:30 Begin Content Module 10–4: The Time Management Process (chapter 10) (1 hour)

Objective: Understand a process to use for time management with specific steps for greater effectiveness.

11:30 Lunch (1 hour)

12:30 p.m. Continue Content Module 10–4: The Time Management Process (chapter 10) (1 hour)

1:30 Break (10 minutes)

1:40   Content Module 10–5: Goal-Setting (chapter 10) (1 hour, 30 minutes)

Objective: Understand the importance of setting goals in relation to time management and steps to take for goal achievement.

3:10   Close (5 minutes)

Objective: Reinforce learning points.

3:15   Participants dismissed.

Sample Agenda Two

This agenda is based on an identified need to improve the ability of learners to manage time more effectively and be aware of their particular behaviors when it comes to time management habits.

TIME

- 8 hours, 5 minutes

MATERIALS

For the instructor:

- Content Module 10–1: Participant Introductions
- Content Module 10–2: Time Management Defined
- Content Module 10–3: Time Management Self-Assessment
- Content Module 10–6: Scheduling Time and Tasks
- Content Module 10–8: Procrastination
- Content Module 10–9: Interruptions and Distractions
- Structured Experience 12–1: Time Management Buddies
- Structured Experience 12–2: A Waste of Time
- Structured Experience 12–6: Getting Around to It
- Structured Experience 12–8: Excuses, Excuses
- Structured Experience 12–9: Interruption Role Play

◆ PowerPoint presentation: Time Management Defined. To access slides for this program, open the file *Time Management Defined.ppt* on the accompanying website. Copies of the slides for this training session are included at the end of chapter 9 (slides 9–1 through 9–10).

◆ PowerPoint presentation: Scheduling Time and Tasks. To access slides for this program, open the file *Scheduling Time and Tasks.ppt* on the accompanying website. Copies of the slides for this training session are included at the end of chapter 9 (slides 9–39 through 9–46).

◆ PowerPoint presentation: Procrastination. To access slides for this program, open the file *Procrastination.ppt* on the accompanying website. Copies of the slides for this training session are included at the end of chapter 9 (slides 9–54 through 9–60).

◆ PowerPoint presentation: Interruptions and Distractions. To access slides for this program, open the file *Interruptions and Distractions.ppt* on the accompanying website. Copies of the slides for this training session are included at the end of chapter 9 (slides 9–61 through 9–70).

For the participants:

◆ Assessment 11–2: Time Management Self-Assessment

◆ Assessment 11–7: Interruptions Self-Assessment

◆ Training Instrument 11–2: Scheduling Sheet

◆ Handout 12–1: Procrastinating Phrases

◆ Handout 12–2: Interruption Role-Play Scenarios

◆ Participants' current schedule of upcoming tasks and appointments or sample tasks and appointments (optional)

◆ Writing instruments and blank paper

SAMPLE AGENDA

8:00 Content Module 10–1: Participant Introductions (chapter 10) (45 minutes; varies by class size)

Objective: Prepare participants to help each other learn.

8:45 Content Module 10–2: Time Management Defined (chapter 10) (1 hour)

Objective: Understand what time management is and the importance of recognizing behaviors that waste time.

9:45   Break (15 minutes)

10:00   Content Module 10–3: Time Management Self-Assessment (chapter 10) (1 hour)

Objective: Identify each participant's highest-impact learning.

11:00   Content Module 10–6: Scheduling Time and Tasks (chapter 10) (1 hour, 15 minutes)

Objective: Learn steps and techniques for scheduling time, and gain practice using a planning tool.

12:15 p.m. Lunch (1 hour)

1:15   Content Module 10–8: Procrastination (chapter 10) (1 hour)

Objective: Explore the many ways people procrastinate and learn techniques to overcome procrastination.

2:15   Break (15 minutes)

2:30   Content Module 10–9: Interruptions and Distractions (chapter 10) (1 hour, 30 minutes)

Objective: Understand the common ways people interrupt others, and practice strategies for managing interruptions and distractions in the workplace.

4:00   Close (5 minutes)

Objective: Reinforce learning points.

4:05   Participants dismissed.

Sample Agenda Three

This agenda is designed to strengthen the time management skills of the participants.

T IME

◆   8 hours

MATERIALS

For the instructor:

- Content Module 10–1: Participant Introductions

- Content Module 10–6: Scheduling Time and Tasks

- Content Module 10–7: Effective Delegation

- Content Module 10–10: Managing Email

- Content Module 10–11: Working With Paperwork

- Structured Experience 12–6: Getting Around to It

- Structured Experience 12–7: Delightful Delegating

- Structured Experience 12–10: Super Subject Lines

- Structured Experience 12–11: Problem Paper

- Structured Experience 12–12: Organization Action Plan

- PowerPoint presentation: Scheduling Time and Tasks. To access slides for this program, open the file *Scheduling Time and Tasks.ppt* on the accompanying website. Copies of the slides for this training session are included at the end of chapter 9 (slides 9–39 through 9–46).

- PowerPoint presentation: Effective Delegation. To access slides for this program, open the file *Effective Delegation.ppt* on the accompanying website. Copies of the slides for this training session are included at the end of chapter 9 (slides 9–47 through 9–53).

- PowerPoint presentation: Managing Email. To access slides for this program, open the file *Managing Email.ppt* on the accompanying website. Copies of the slides for this training session are included at the end of chapter 9 (slides 9–71 through 9–80).

- PowerPoint presentation: Working With Paperwork. To access slides for this program, open the file *Working With Paperwork.ppt* on the accompanying website. Copies of the slides for this training session are included at the end of chapter 9 (slides 9–81 through 9–92).

- Materials for small groups to sort provided by the facilitator (such as scribbled meeting notes, magazine articles, business memos, sample invoices, training handouts, party invitations, and sample reports)

- Blank slips of paper or sticky notes

For the participants:

- ◆ Training Instrument 11–2: Scheduling Sheet

- ◆ Training Instrument 11–3: Organization Action Plan

- ◆ Handout 12–3: Subject Line Practice

- ◆ Handout 12–4: Paperwork Samples

- ◆ Participants' current schedule of upcoming tasks and appointments or sample tasks and appointments (optional)

- ◆ Writing instruments and blank paper

SAMPLE AGENDA

8:00 a.m.   Content Module 10–1: Participant Introductions (chapter 10) (45 minutes; varies by class size)

Objective: Prepare participants to help each other learn.

8:45   Content Module 10–6: Scheduling Time and Tasks (chapter 10) (1 hour, 15 minutes)

Objective: Learn steps and techniques for scheduling time, and gain practice using a planning tool.

10:00   Break (15 minutes)

10:15   Content Module 10–7: Effective Delegation (chapter 10) (1 hour, 15 minutes)

Objective: Identify current behaviors for delegating, and learn strategies to delegate more for lower stress and increased focus.

11:30   Lunch (1 hour)

12:30 p.m.   Content Module 10–10: Managing Email (chapter 10) (1 hour, 15 minutes)

Objective: Learn techniques and etiquette for working with email that lead to better productivity and efficiency with less frustration.

1:45   Break (10 minutes)

1:55	Content Module 10–11: Working With Paperwork (chapter 10) (2 hours)
	Objective: Understand and practice simple steps to deal with clutter and effectively manage paper in the office.
3:55	Close (5 minutes)
	Objective: Reinforce learning points.
4:00	Participants dismissed.

Step-by-Step Planning

Just before the training session:

- Arrive at the facility early.

- Set up and test equipment (laptop, projector, and flipcharts).

- Confirm refreshments.

At the training session:

- Introduce yourself to the participants. Include a description of your role in the training process, as well as your training and work experience. First impressions count, and this is your chance to establish credibility with the participants.

- If you do not use the participant introductions exercise, ask the participants to introduce themselves by sharing their names, roles, and what they would like to gain from the training. Let them know they will be helping each other learn.

- Review the agenda and learning objectives with the participants.

- Go through the selected content modules.

- Ask for questions and test for understanding frequently.

- Close the session with an opportunity for the participants to ask questions. If appropriate, offer your help and availability on an ongoing basis.

What to Do Next

- ◆ Identify the training participants and assess their most critical training needs, or identify the competencies the organization seeks to develop.

- ◆ Determine the agenda based on the highest value content modules called for by your needs assessment or the required competencies.

- ◆ Schedule the session.

- ◆ Arrange a facility for the training session.

- ◆ Invite participants. Check for any special dietary needs.

- ◆ Send a confirmation to participants. Include an agenda and any pre-work with the confirmation.

- ◆ Prepare training materials (handouts, overheads, presentations, and exercise materials).

- ◆ Order food and beverages.

◆

Multi-Day Session

What's in This Chapter?

- ◆ Advice on choosing the content for training sessions

- ◆ Step-by-step preparation and training delivery instructions

- ◆ Sample agendas

The materials in this book have been designed to meet a variety of training needs and timeframes, and this chapter covers designs suitable for day-and-a-half and two-day training sessions.

As noted in chapter 8, longer learning experiences might raise concerns that participants will be overloaded with information. To avoid this, design programs that allow participants to learn efficiently and at their own pace. The purpose of this chapter is to present a significant amount of content in a multi-day session by mixing short, to-the-point theory and models with experiential exercises and assessments. This keeps the participants from feeling overwhelmed and, instead, produces an enjoyable, fruitful learning experience. In addition, there are important benefits associated with extended learning experiences. Although a shorter program might be seen as part of a typical workday, a longer program can become a memorable life experience for the participant, particularly if it is held at an offsite venue and includes an overnight stay. A multi-day design provides ample opportunity to create the learning environment (as discussed in chapter 4) and establish participants as learning partners. Discussion during breaks, meals, and evening activities often provides valuable feedback and learning. It often takes a different physical environment and a complete break from daily routine for participants to focus on learning.

Multi-day sessions are appropriate for group training. The backgrounds and experiences of a variety of participants create and enrich the learning environment. For multi-day sessions, a group of 12 to 24 participants is best. Smaller groups can limit the richness of group interactions, and larger groups can become unwieldy for the facilitator and can depersonalize the learning experience.

Please note that although illustrative designs are included, the trainer should adapt them to fit his or her specific purposes. Each design can be modified to consider the resources available, the learning readiness of potential participants, and especially the assessed development needs of the target audience.

Objectives and Use

The objectives of a multi-day training session are to free participants from their daily routines so they can understand the learning content that is of greatest value, as well as build relationships between the trainer and the participants. The group setting and time available for interaction allow for rich and diverse discussion of the various topics.

Note: Residential programs held at appealing offsite facilities can also be used to create a special learning experience.

A multi-day training session is appropriate for the following circumstances:

- ◆ The targeted, available audience for training is 12 or more.

- ◆ The targeted audience requires comprehensive training in all relevant content areas.

- ◆ Training facilities for groups are available.

- ◆ Participants are available for multiple days.

- ◆ Funding for meals, and possibly for an offsite location, is available.

Choosing the Content

Any of the content modules in this book can be used for multi-day training sessions. Although a multi-day session allows time to cover all of the content modules, you may still need to perform a needs assessment of the participant group or review the competencies the organization seeks to develop. Include only those modules indicated by your needs assessment.

With a session that covers multiple days, you've crossed over the meal and possibly the overnight thresholds. Hunger and thirst are enemies of the learning environment, so offer beverages, snacks, and meals at the breaks, so your participants' biological needs are met. Keep participants together during meals to encourage continued discussion of learning points. It also helps to strengthen the relationships between participants and, therefore, helps support the learning environment. Much discussion and feedback occurs during dinner after a long day of training. As noted in chapter 8, scheduled meals discourage participants from going back to the office and getting distracted from their learning focus. It also helps to keep your session on schedule because participants are less likely to come back late from the lunch break.

All the content modules in this book are included in one of the following sample agendas. The timing of the modules assumes that all of the structured experiences will be included.

The placement of the "Participant Introductions," "Time Management Defined," and "Time Management Self-Assessment" modules is important. Offer these modules at the beginning of the session because they help focus participants' learning by creating the context for the remaining content modules.

Sample Agenda, Day One

TIME

◆ 11 + hours

MATERIALS

For the instructor:

- ◆ Content Module 10–1: Participant Introductions

- ◆ Content Module 10–2: Time Management Defined

- ◆ Content Module 10–3: Time Management Self-Assessment

- ◆ Content Module 10–4: The Time Management Process

- ◆ Content Module 10–5: Goal-Setting

- ◆ Structured Experience 12–1: Time Management Buddies

◆ Structured Experience 12–2: A Waste of Time

◆ Structured Experience 12–3: Roles and Responsibilities

◆ Structured Experience 12–4: Where Does the Time Go?

◆ Structured Experience 12–5: Goal-Setting Practice

◆ PowerPoint presentation: Time Management Defined. To access slides for this program, open the file *Time Management Defined.ppt* on the accompanying website. Copies of the slides for this training session are included at the end of this chapter (slides 9–1 through 9–10).

◆ PowerPoint presentation: The Time Management Process. To access slides for this program, open the file *The Time Management Process.ppt* on the accompanying website. Copies of the slides for this training session are included at the end of this chapter (slides 9–11 through 9–28).

◆ PowerPoint presentation: Goal-Setting. To access slides for this program, open the file *Goal-Setting.ppt* on the accompanying website. Copies of the slides for this training session are included at the end of this chapter (slides 9–29 through 9–38).

For the participants:

◆ Assessment 11–2: Time Management Self-Assessment

◆ Training Instrument 11–1: Goal-Setting Worksheet

◆ Participants' printouts of last week's calendar and task list, pages from a planner, or information on a personal digital assistant

◆ Writing instruments and blank paper

SAMPLE AGENDA

8:00 a.m.   Content Module 10–1: Participant Introductions (chapter 10) (45 minutes; varies by class size)

Objective: Prepare participants to help each other learn.

8:45   Content Module 10–2: Time Management Defined (chapter 10) (1 hour, 30 minutes)

Objective: Understand what time management is and the importance of recognizing behaviors that waste time.

10:15	Break (15 minutes)
10:30	Content Module 10–3: Time Management Self-Assessment (chapter 10) (1 hour)
	Objective: Identify each participant's highest-impact learning.
11:30	Begin Content Module 10–4: The Time Management Process (chapter 10) (1 hour)
	Objective: Understand a process to use for time management with specific steps for greater effectiveness.
12:30 p.m.	Lunch (1 hour)
1:30	Continue Content Module 10–4: The Time Management Process (1 hour)
2:30	Break (15 minutes)
2:45	Content Module 10–5: Goal-Setting (chapter 10) (1 hour, 30 minutes)
	Objective: Understand the importance of setting goals in relation to time management and steps to take for goal achievement.
4:15	Close (5 minutes)
	Objective: Reinforce learning points.
4:20	Break (1 hour, 40 minutes)
6:00	Dinner (if at an offsite location)
7:00	After-dinner activities (if at a residential offsite location)

Sample Agenda, Day Two (Full-Day Option)

TIME

◆ 8 hours, 35 minutes

MATERIALS

For the instructor:

- ◆ Content Module 10–6: Scheduling Time and Tasks

- ◆ Content Module 10–7: Effective Delegation

- Content Module 10–8: Procrastination

- Content Module 10–9: Interruptions and Distractions

- Content Module 10–11: Working With Paperwork

- Structured Experience 12–6: Getting Around to It

- Structured Experience 12–7: Delightful Delegating

- Structured Experience 12–8: Excuses, Excuses

- Structured Experience 12–9: Interruption Role Play

- Structured Experience 12–11: Problem Paper

- Structured Experience 12–12: Organization Action Plan

- PowerPoint presentation: Scheduling Time and Tasks. To access slides for this program, open the file *Scheduling Time and Tasks.ppt* on the accompanying website. Copies of the slides for this training session are included at the end of this chapter (slides 9–39 through 9–46).

- PowerPoint presentation: Effective Delegation. To access slides for this program, open the file *Effective Delegation.ppt* on the accompanying website. Copies of the slides for this training session are included at the end of this chapter (slides 9–47 through 9–53).

- PowerPoint presentation: Procrastination. To access slides for this program, open the file *Procrastination.ppt* on the accompanying website. Copies of the slides for this training session are included at the end of this chapter (slides 9–54 through 9–60).

- PowerPoint presentation: Interruptions and Distractions. To access slides for this program, open the file *Interruptions and Distractions.ppt* on the accompanying website. Copies of the slides for this training session are included at the end of this chapter (slides 9–61 through 9–70).

- PowerPoint presentation: Working With Paperwork. To access slides for this program, open the file *Working With Paperwork.ppt* on the accompanying website. Copies of the slides for this training session are included at the end of this chapter (slides 9–81 through 9–92).

- Materials for small groups to sort provided by the facilitator (such as scribbled meeting notes, magazine articles, business memos, sample invoices, training handouts, party invitations, and sample reports)

- Blank slips of paper or sticky notes

For the participants:

- ◆ Assessment 11–7: Interruptions Self-Assessment

- ◆ Training Instrument 11–2: Scheduling Sheet

- ◆ Training Instrument 11–3: Organization Action Plan

- ◆ Handout 12–1: Procrastinating Phrases

- ◆ Handout 12–2: Interruption Role-Play Scenarios

- ◆ Handout 12–4: Paperwork Samples

- ◆ Participants' current schedule of upcoming tasks and appointments or sample tasks and appointments (optional)

- ◆ Writing instruments and blank paper

SAMPLE AGENDA

8:00 a.m.   Content Module 10–6: Scheduling Time and Tasks (chapter 10) (1 hour, 15 minutes)

Objective: Learn steps and techniques for scheduling time, and gain practice using a planning tool.

9:15   Break (15 minutes)

9:30   Content Module 10–7: Effective Delegation (chapter 10) (1 hour, 15 minutes)

Objective: Identify current behaviors for delegating, and learn strategies to delegate more for lowered stress and increased focus.

10:45   Content Module 10–8: Procrastination (chapter 10) (1 hour)

Objective: Explore the many ways people procrastinate, and learn techniques to overcome procrastination.

11:45   Lunch (1 hour)

12:45 p.m.   Content Module 10–9: Interruptions and Distractions (chapter 10) (1 hour, 30 minutes)

Objective: Understand the common ways people interrupt others, and practice strategies for managing interruptions and distractions in the workplace.

2:15   Break (15 minutes)

2:30   Content Module 10–11: Working With Paperwork (chapter 10) (2 hours)

        Objective: Understand and practice simple steps to deal with clutter and effectively manage paper in the office.

4:30   Close (5 minutes)

        Objective: Reinforce learning points.

4:35   Participants dismissed.

Sample Agenda, Day Two (Half-Day Option)

TIME

◆ 3 hours, 35 minutes

MATERIALS

For the instructor:

◆ Content Module 10–10: Managing Email

◆ Content Module 10–11: Working With Paperwork

◆ Structured Experience 12–10: Super Subject Lines

◆ Structured Experience 12–11: Problem Paper

◆ Structured Experience 12–12: Organization Action Plan

◆ PowerPoint presentation: Managing Email. To access slides for this program, open the file *Managing Email.ppt* on the accompanying website. Copies of the slides for this training session are included at the end of this chapter (slides 9–71 through 9–80).

◆ PowerPoint presentation: Working With Paperwork. To access slides for this program, open the file *Working With Paperwork.ppt* on the accompanying website. Copies of the slides for this training session are included at the end of this chapter (slides 9–81 through 9–92).

- Materials for small groups to sort provided by the facilitator (such as scribbled meeting notes, magazine articles, business memos, sample invoices, training handouts, party invitations, and sample reports)

- Blank slips of paper or sticky notes

For the participants:

- Training Instrument 11–3: Organization Action Plan

- Handout 12–3: Subject Line Practice

- Handout 12–4: Paperwork Samples

- Writing instruments

SAMPLE AGENDA

8:00 a.m.	Content Module 10–10: Managing Email (chapter 10) (1 hour, 15 minutes)
	Objective: Learn techniques and etiquette for working with email that lead to better productivity and efficiency with less frustration.
9:15	Break (15 minutes)
9:30	Content Module 10–11: Working With Paperwork (chapter 10) (2 hours)
	Objective: Understand and practice simple steps to deal with clutter and effectively manage paper in the office.
11:30	Close (5 minutes)
	Objective: Reinforce learning points.
11:35	Participants dismissed.

Step-by-Step Planning

Just before the training session:

- If this is a residential program, confirm room arrangements with hotel.

- Arrive at the facility early.

◆ Set up and test equipment (laptop, projector, and flipcharts).

◆ Confirm refreshments.

At the training session:

◆ Introduce yourself to the participants. Include a description of your role in the training process, as well as your training and work experience. First impressions count, and this is your chance to establish credibility with the participants.

◆ If you do not use the participant introductions exercise, ask the participants to introduce themselves by sharing their names, roles, and what they would like to gain from the training. Let them know they will be helping each other learn.

◆ Review each day's agenda and learning objectives with the participants.

◆ Go through the selected content modules.

◆ Ask for questions and test for understanding frequently.

◆ Close each day with an opportunity for the participants to ask questions.

What to Do Next

◆ Identify the training participants and assess their most critical training needs, or identify the competencies the organization seeks to develop.

◆ Design the agenda based on the highest value content modules called for by your needs assessment or the required competencies.

◆ Schedule the session.

◆ Arrange a facility for the training session. Book a block of rooms if this is a residential program.

◆ Invite participants. Check for any special dietary needs. If this is a residential program, check for room requirements (such as smoking or nonsmoking and single or double bed).

◆ Send a confirmation to participants. Include an agenda and any prework with the confirmation.

◆ Prepare training materials (handouts, overheads, presentations, and exercise materials).

◆ Order food and beverages.

Slide 9–1

Time Management Defined

Lisa J. Downs

American Society for Training &
Development

Slide 9–2

To Manage Time Is To...

- Use time effectively to achieve desired results.
- Understand how we spend our time.
- Use tools and processes for efficiency and productivity.

Slide 9–3

Time Management Principles

- Focus on importance, not urgency.
- Make conscious choices about what to do when.
- Learn to say "no."
- Develop a personalized system for managing time.

Slide 9–4

Why Time Management?

- Improves work-life balance
- Leads to increased productivity
- Lowers stress levels
- Creates more time for what's important
- Develops delegation and organizational skills
- Enables goal achievement

Slide 9–5

Common Time Wasters

- Procrastination
- Unnecessary meetings
- Interruptions
- Internet surfing
- Trivial emails
- Paperwork

Slide 9–6

Did You Know?

The average adult spends 50–70% of the work day dealing with paper.

What are the implications of this for time management?

Slide 9–7

Why Do We Waste Time?

- Stressed out
- Overworked
- Overwhelmed
- Exhausted
- Disorganized
- Unfocused

Time wasters = escape

Slide 9–8

Steps to Time Management

- Prioritizing
- Analyzing
- Filtering
- Scheduling
- Executing

Slide 9–9

Keep in Mind...

- Time management is a personalized process, unique for each individual.
- When done effectively, good time management should make you feel energized, focused, and balanced.

Slide 9–10

Consider...

"Time is the coin of your life. It is the only coin you have, and only you can determine how it will be spent."

– *Carl Sandburg*

How do you interpret this idea?

Slide 9–11

The Time Management Process

Lisa J. Downs

American Society for Training & Development

Slide 9–12

Needs Fulfilled by Time Management

- To feel more in control of our lives
- To make the most of every day
- To accomplish what we set out to do

Slide 9–13

Step 1: Prioritizing

- Focus on roles and responsibilities at work and at home.

- Ask yourself, "What is most important for me to be doing at this time?"

- Devote less energy to noncritical tasks.

- Know what your work actually is and what is involved.

Slide 9–14

Model for Reviewing Work

- 50,000+ feet: Life as a whole

- 40,000 feet: 3- to 5-year vision

- 30,000 feet: 1- to 2-year goals

- 20,000 feet: Areas of responsibility

- 10,000 feet: Current projects

- Ground level: Current actions

Source: Allen, David. *Getting Things Done*. New York, NY: Penguin Group, 2001.

Slide 9–15

Model for Reviewing Work (cont'd.)

- 50,000 feet: What is the purpose of your work?

- 40,000 feet: What will you be doing 3–5 years from now?

- 30,000 feet: What will you accomplish 1–2 years out?

Slide 9–16

Model for Reviewing Work (cont'd.)

- 20,000 feet: In what key areas do you want to achieve results?

- 10,000 feet: What are the short-term projects that must be done?

- Ground level: What actions are needed to focus on these projects?

Slide 9–17

Step 2: Analyzing

- Look closely at where you are spending your time.

- Make an effort to analyze your days.

- Log your time for one week.

- Search for pockets of time, items to cut, time of day tasks are done, pace of work.

- Adjust scheduling and routines as needed.

Slide 9–18

Questions to Ask

- How are most of your hours spent?

- Is your schedule in balance (work, family, time for self)?

- Did anything from your log surprise you?

- Is there any time you cannot account for?

- How do you decide what to spend your time doing?

Slide 9–19

Step 3: Filtering

- Keep in mind that we cannot find time; we have to make it by taking it away from other activities.

- Remember that the easiest option is not always the best.

- Consider if the action is what you *want* or *need* to be doing right now; if not, say "no."

Slide 9–20

Filtering Categories

1. Urgent and Important: Needs immediate attention and aligns with priorities

2. Important but Not Urgent: No sense of immediacy, but must be done

3. Urgent but Not Important: Not tied to priorities; involves others' urgencies

4. Neither Important nor Urgent: Time wasters

Source: Cook, Marshall J. *Time Management*. Avon, MA: Adams Media, 1998.

Slide 9–21

Filtering Categories (cont'd.)

1. Urgent and Important:
   - Child sick at school
   - Presentation at meeting in 1 hour
   - Fell and hurt yourself

2. Important but Not Urgent:
   - Long-range budgeting
   - Time with family
   - Continuing education

Slide 9–22

Filtering Categories (cont'd.)

3. Urgent but Not Important
   - Colleague showing you vacation photos
   - Email pop-up box
   - Department meeting in 10 minutes

4. Neither Important nor Urgent:
   - Surfing the Internet
   - Doing the crossword puzzle in the paper
   - Checking sports scores

Slide 9–23

Step 4: Scheduling

- Involves creating a plan of action for your days, weeks, and months

- Makes use of organizational tools: planner, PDA, scheduling software, lists

- Assists with focus on important tasks and responsibilities aligned with priorities

- Allows for flexibility as needs change

Slide 9–24

Scheduling Tips

- Record to-do items in one reliable location.

- Overestimate how long tasks will take.

- Avoid over-booking to allow for interruptions and unexpected urgencies.

- Keep things in perspective.

- Find a format that works for you and that allows for flexibility.

Slide 9–25

Scheduling Tips (cont'd.)

- Make sure important tasks get done first.
- Break large tasks down into pieces.
- Schedule for long term and short term.
- Build in breaks for yourself.
- Be ready to "let it go" if necessary; not all days will go according to plan.

Slide 9–26

Step 5: Executing

- Taking action based on plans and priorities
- Taking charge of your time and schedule
- Acknowledging where and when time wasters occur and taking steps to eliminate them
- Using goals, roles, and responsibilities to drive productivity

Slide 9–27

Executing: Saying "No"

Say "no" when

- Meetings are ineffective or unnecessary
- New projects are misaligned with goals or resources
- Tasks are a waste of time; look for alternative actions
- You are not the right person for the task
- You need to focus.

Slide 9–28

Self-Management

- Time cannot be saved or stored.
- We must manage ourselves in relation to time.
- It is the way we use time that matters, not how much we have.
- Any bad habits must be changed to better control our use of time.

Slide 9–29

Goal-Setting

Lisa J. Downs

American Society of Training & Development

Slide 9–30

The Purpose of Goals

- To act as a compass—point the way
- To help us prioritize activities
- To boost our sense of accomplishment and satisfaction

Slide 9–31

Types of Goals

- Critical goals: must be accomplished to be successful

- Enabling goals: fulfill a long-term, but not immediate, need

- Nice-to-have goals: improvements to enhance your life or work, but not crucial

Source: Roberto, Michael. *Time Management*. Boston, MA: Harvard Business School Publishing, 2005.

Slide 9–32

Types of Goals (cont'd.)

- Critical goal: Improve profitability within two years.

- Enabling goal: Update marketing materials to recruit new employees.

- Nice-to-have goal: Improve catering choices for company events.

Slide 9–33

Goal-Setting Tips

- Record goals in specific terms; avoid being vague.

- Put a timeframe around goal achievement.

- Decide how progress will be measured.

- Align goals with important priorities and strategies.

- Stretch yourself, but don't overdo it.

Slide 9–34

Goal-Setting Steps

1. Create a list of major life roles or categories, such as family, work, self, finances, community, etc.

2. Next to each category, write down what you see yourself doing in 10 years; these statements are your long-term goals.

3. Break each goal down into smaller pieces by recording two or three specific actions next to each statement.

Slide 9–35

Goal-Setting Steps (cont'd.)

4. Create smaller tasks from the specific actions.

5. Schedule these tasks into your planning system.

6. Review your goals and activities a minimum of once a year; revise as needed.

Slide 9–36

An Example...

Category: Self

10 Years from Now: "I will have my MBA degree."

Specific Activities: Research MBA programs.

Decide timing.

Investigate funding.

What tasks should now be scheduled?

Slide 9–37

Goal Alignment

- If working in an organization, goals should cascade down.

- Department or team goals should align with company goals.

- Individual goals should align with department or team goals.

Slide 9–38

Importance of Goals

- Effective time management starts with having clearly defined goals.

- Goals give us purpose and a road map to guide us.

- When goals are in writing, opportunities follow.

Slide 9–39

Scheduling Time and Tasks

Lisa J. Downs

American Society for Training & Development

Slide 9–40

Scheduling Tips

- Group or "chunk" similar tasks together for clarity and focus (e.g., returning phone calls).

- Organize tasks and appointments on one page to see at a glance what has to be done.

- If you add a task to a "to-do" list, take something out to avoid overload.

- Calculate how long tasks will take you to accomplish.

Slide 9–41

Calculating Task Time

- For one week, note in your planning system how long you *think* it will take to do a task.

- Then log the *actual* time it took to complete the same task.

- Compare the estimates to the actual time—is there a pattern? Are the gaps off by the same amount?

- Use the time estimates to block out time as accurately as possible.

Slide 9–42

Common Hidden Time Costs

- Interruptions

- Set up and tear down time for presentations, displays, etc.

- Travel time

- Unexpected problems

- Personal time—eating, breaks, restroom, etc.

- Time to think

Slide 9–43

Meeting Deadlines

To schedule time for large projects:

- Back time milestone tasks from the deadline (what needs to be done 1 week out, 2 weeks out, 1 month out, etc.).
- Schedule work in smaller segments.
- Block out 1–2 hours of work time ("blocks") on your calendar.
- Minimize distractions.

Slide 9–44

Multitasking

- Adults are able to do a variety of tasks any given day; however, we can only do *one* thing very well at *one* time.
- Focus for just 15 minutes on *only one* task at a time to boost productivity.
- Gradually increase the time you focus on one task to 30, 45, and then to 60 minutes, and watch your productivity rise.

Slide 9–45

Scheduling Steps

1. Visualize how your day/week will go and what will be accomplished.
2. Do your planning at the same time every day to form the habit.
3. Decide for what period of time you will schedule—daily, weekly, or whatever is appropriate.
4. Review uncompleted items, projects, and goals.

Slide 9–46

Scheduling Steps (Cont'd.)

5. Review appointments.
6. Prioritize tasks using ABCs (A = most important, B = middle importance, C = least important).
7. Block off time on particular dates for major activities, using your priorities as a guide.
8. Check off items as they are completed for clarity and a sense of accomplishment.

Slide 9–47

Effective Delegation

Lisa J. Downs

American Society for Training & Development

Slide 9–48

Why Delegate?

- Reduces your workload and stress level
- Provides more time to focus on the important
- Builds trust among team members and an understanding of others
- Broadens opportunities for staff members
- Empowers others to contribute and make good decisions

Slide 9–49

Delegating Skills May Need Improvement If...

- You are regularly putting in extra hours on tasks "only you can do"
- You second-guess direct reports' decisions and rework their assigned tasks
- You intervene in projects assigned to others
- Morale is low and turnover is high
- Your inbox is always filled to capacity.

Slide 9–50

Guidelines for Delegating

- Be clear about what you want done, when it should be done, and the expected results.
- Delegate both tedious and interesting tasks.
- Be prepared to do some coaching if needed.
- Monitor progress (schedule dates) and provide feedback.
- Keep lines of communication open, to be available as a resource.

Slide 9–51

Guidelines for Delegating (Cont'd.)

- Build a shared sense of responsibility among the team.
- Focus on *results*, not on how tasks should be accomplished.
- Develop trust in less-skilled staff by providing structured assignments.
- Develop strong performers by assigning projects with high visibility.

Slide 9–52

Assigning the Work

- Match the right person with the task.
- Clearly describe the task or project and how it fits into the big picture.
- Identify roles and responsibilities for the work.
- Discuss deadlines and resources.
- Establish standards of performance and accountability.

Slide 9–53

Post-Work Review

When the assignment is complete

- Ask the employee how it went
- Provide positive reinforcement for work done well
- Use ongoing coaching or training as necessary
- Seek employees' input on their interests for future projects.

Slide 9–54

Procrastination

Lisa J. Downs

American Society for Training & Development

Slide 9–55

Defining Procrastination

- Procrastination is the postponing of activities, often at an excessive level.
- Procrastination results in wasted time, missed opportunities, low performance, and high stress.

Slide 9–56

Why People Procrastinate

- Fear of failure
- Perfectionism
- Negative self-talk—inadequacy
- Don't know where to start
- Unpleasant task
- Distraction—lack of focus

Slide 9–57

Phrases of Procrastination

Do any of these thoughts seem familiar?
- "I've got to start soon."
- "I should have started earlier."
- "There's still time."
- "Why bother? I can't finish it anyway."
- "I will not do this to myself again."

Slide 9–58

Habit of Procrastination

- Realize that procrastinating is a habit; a new habit will take time to develop.
- Understand the cause, then develop strategies to fix it; seek help if needed.
- Work on both the task and the environmental aspects of harmful procrastination.

Slide 9–59

Strategies: Tasks

- Complete unpleasant tasks first, early in the day.
- Break large jobs into smaller pieces.
- Determine a time to make a decision and share the deadline with others.
- Reward yourself for accomplishments.
- Do something—no matter how small.

Slide 9–60

Strategies: Environment

- Close your door and clean up clutter.
- Remove food, magazines, and other distractions from the work space.
- Tell your co-workers you are not to be disturbed for the block of time you are working.
- Put a reminder to focus where you will see it.

Slide 9–61

Interruptions and Distractions

Lisa J. Downs

American Society for Training & Development

Slide 9–62

Common Distractions

- People stopping by to visit
- Phone calls
- Email (pop-up notification boxes)
- Office parties/events
- Hunger
- Fatigue
- Anxiety or stress

Slide 9–63

Preventing Interruptions

- Isolate yourself—close the door, put up a sign, or work in a conference room. If possible, work remotely.
- Don't feel obligated to keep an "open door." Open door does not equal "always available"; it means open communication.
- Inform others of your workflow and availability.

Slide 9–64

Preventing Interruptions (Cont'd.)

- If you have an assistant, establish guidelines of when interruptions are OK.
- Change the location of your desk, if possible, if it faces office traffic.
- Move any materials or files used by others to another area, if possible.
- Block off time for work on priorities.

Slide 9–65

Tips for "Walk-Ins"

- When someone asks for your time, suggest a specific time later in the day.
- If it is urgent (to them), ask how many minutes they need and stick to it.
- Stand up; it prevents someone from getting comfortable.
- Place items on visitors' chairs or remove the chairs altogether.

Slide 9–66

Tips for "Walk-Ins" (Cont'd.)

- Ask direct reports to save up a list of items for discussion and deal with them at an appointed time.
- If telling stories, ask the person to sum up what they need from you.
- If asking for help, ask the person what solution they propose.

Slide 9–67

Handling Distractions

- Use a reminder that you will see: "Is What I'm Doing Right Now Aligned With My Goals?"
- Send calls to voicemail when needed.
- Turn off the pop-up box for email notification or minimize email window.
- Clear your desk of unnecessary items.

Slide 9–68

Handling Distractions (Cont'd.)

- If in a cubicle, use headphones, if allowed, to block out noise.
- Hang a "do not disturb" sign and/or notify co-workers of when you need to focus.
- Avoid unnecessary meetings and attending noncritical office events.
- Coach direct reports, but don't assume their problems.

Slide 9–69

Saying "No"

- Stick to your plan.
- When someone persists, repeat your position in a slightly different way.
- Be sure to understand what's asked of you before responding.
- Remember, you have a right to say "no."
- Be polite, but firm.

Slide 9–70

Saying "No" to Your Boss

- Remind your supervisor of other projects you have; ask for help with prioritizing.
- Point out that although you might be able to do everything, it may not be up to usual standards.
- Provide suggestions or alternatives to solve the problem or issue.

Slide 9–71

Managing Email

Lisa J. Downs

American Society for Training & Development

Slide 9–72

Email Productivity Tips

- Minimize the distraction of a pop-up box by shutting it off or setting it to check every hour.
- Take action on each email: delete it, file it, or reply/act.
- Use templates and autoresponders for standard messages.

Slide 9–73

Email Productivity Tips (Cont'd.)

- Turn emails into calendar appointments or tasks; avoid using your inbox as a "to-do" list.
- Write less text; keep messages short and to the point.
- Focus on easy emails with quick replies first.

Slide 9–74

Email Productivity Tips (Cont'd.)

- Use rules to automatically send certain messages into designated folders.
- Designate blocks of time in your schedule to check email; start with 3–4 times a day and gradually reduce it to 2–3 times.

Slide 9–75

Effective Email Formatting

- Proofread your emails before sending.
- Use copy and paste commands as you would in word processing to save time.
- Write descriptive subject lines with calls to action to catch attention and for ease of filing.

Slide 9–76

Effective Email Formatting (Cont'd.)

- If forwarding a message, put your comments at the top for clarity.
- Use "bcc" for bulk emails and be careful to reply to only the person you intend.
- Avoid unnecessary punctuation and acronyms.

Slide 9–77

Keep in Mind...

- The more you follow good email formatting and etiquette, the more likely you will receive it in return; this increases efficiency.
- Setting expectations is important; get others in the habit of knowing when you will be processing your email.

Slide 9–78

Additional Time Savers

- Use a tray on your desk for paper items associated with email you want to send; label this accordingly.
- Sort incoming messages by subject or author to process related email together.

Slide 9–79

Additional Time Savers (Cont'd.)

- Unsubscribe or remove your email address from unwanted or unread mailings.

- Keep an address book to save email addresses.

- Delete messages with attachments after you save them to your hard drive; they take up a lot of server space and this will prevent future problems.

Slide 9–80

Points to Remember

- *You* control your email: when you process it, how you use it, and setting these expectations with others.

- By checking email only at certain times of the day, you may find that many issues will be resolved on their own.

Slide 9–81

Working With Paperwork

Lisa J. Downs

American Society for Training & Development

Slide 9–82

Questions to Ask Yourself

- Can I *really* find what I need quickly and can someone else find it if necessary?

- Is my work environment slowing me down or making me feel out of control?

- Do I feel overwhelmed by paper?

Slide 9–83

Our Sources of Clutter

- A nesting instinct: Things provide a sense of security and comfort.

- Messy = creative: In reality, a mess is costing you time.

- Chronic saving: You never know when you might need it.

Slide 9–84

The Paperwork Process

Step 1: Sort items into categories.

Step 2: Take action: File, delegate, or toss.

Step 3: Maintain a paperwork routine.

Slide 9–85

Sorting

- If overwhelming, start with small chunks of time: 15 minutes, 30 minutes, etc.

- Stand up while sorting; this increases efficiency with a sense of urgency.

- Touch each item only once and make a quick decision.

Slide 9–86

Taking Action

- If a piece of paper only needs a brief response, do it now.

- Schedule a short filing session once a day, week, or month.

- If a more thoughtful response is required, schedule a task.

Slide 9–87

Filing Documents

- Keep hanging file tabs on one side of the folder only, for easy scanning.

- Create different file folders: reading, to-do, vendors, invoices, upcoming events, etc, and store them in a wire rack for easy access.

Slide 9–88

Maintaining a Routine

- Block out time for dealing with clutter: 15 minutes a day, one hour a week, etc.

- Use files, containers, and other desk accessories for easy organization.

- Ask, "Do I really want or need this?"

Slide 9–89

Tips to Handle Paperwork

- Carry a notebook with you at all times to prevent having loose pieces of paper.

- Create files immediately and keep an accessible file cabinet close by.

- Keep supplies for rerouting and recycling handy.

Slide 9–90

Tips to Handle Paperwork (Cont'd.)

- Ask to be taken off of unnecessary mailing lists and subscriptions.

- Clip useful material from periodicals and toss the rest.

- Skim and scan reading material; schedule reading for twice a week.

Slide 9–91

Tips to Handle Paperwork (Cont'd.)

- Ask, "How valuable is this information?"
- Toss envelopes right away.
- Toss old drafts of documents.
- Throw out the previous month's magazine when the new one arrives.

Slide 9–92

Tips to Handle Paperwork (Cont'd.)

- Ask subordinates to limit the number and length of written reports.
- Cut back on sending and keeping memos; call instead.
- Enter business contacts into a database; toss business cards when done.

◆

Content Modules

- ◆ Detailed instructions for using the content modules

- ◆ Content Modules 10–1 through 10–11

This chapter contains all of the content modules that appear in the sample agendas found in previous chapters. The term *content* refers to the emphases within the modules. Each content module is a self-contained learning experience that can be used as a stand-alone training session or incorporated into a broader agenda. Designed to explore content areas interactively in a step-by-step fashion, the content modules are handy, readily available resources to help facilitators address the issues that learners face in effective time management training.

Using the Content Modules

These content modules are the building blocks of a training program for negotiators. Each module includes, as appropriate:

- ◆ Step-by-step instructions

- ◆ Key learning points

- ◆ Discussion questions

- ◆ List of materials to be used in each module, including

    - ◆ Training instruments

   ◆ PowerPoint presentations

   ◆ Structured exercises

Trainers should review the content module that they plan to facilitate, along with all of the resources used in the module. After becoming familiar with the content, a trainer should follow the step-by-step instructions given in the module. Time estimates are provided for each module and each step, but the time needed for each activity may vary with different facilitators and participants.

A trainer can modify these modules to comply with the organization's priorities, the readiness level of potential participants, or the resources available in terms of time, space, and availability of trainees. These modules apply many of the principles of adult learning specified in chapter 3 of this book. The trainer should understand and be committed to these principles before revising the step-by-step approaches included here.

The Modules

The designs included in this chapter emphasize learning through doing, using the materials in this book. As recommended in chapter 2, the trainer should conduct a needs assessment before he or she decides which modules will be used, how they will be modified, and how to combine various modules into longer sessions.

Here are the 11 modules in this section:

   ◆ **Content Module 10–1: Participant Introductions.** This module helps create a collaborative learning environment by introducing participants to each other and showing them that each person's role is to contribute to the learning process.

   ◆ **Content Module 10–2: Time Management Defined.** The phrase *time management* may be ambiguous for some people. This module clarifies what it means to manage time, the importance of recognizing good time management, and common ways to avoid wasting time.

   ◆ **Content Module 10–3: Time Management Self-Assessment.** This module helps participants assess their strengths and weaknesses in managing time, and it explores how poor time management can negatively affect our work with others, as well as individual productivity and efficiency.

◆ **Content Module 10–4: The Time Management Process.** In this module, a five-step process for effective time management includes ways to set priorities and analyze how time is currently spent, as well as strategies to filter information and handle demands on our time as they are presented.

◆ **Content Module 10–5: Goal-Setting.** This module explains techniques that will help learners set and achieve goals and identify priorities to gain focus.

◆ **Content Module 10–6: Scheduling Time and Tasks.** This module helps participants understand some of the tools available for scheduling, and it provides tips to help plan when tasks will be completed.

◆ **Content Module 10–7: Effective Delegation.** Positive and negative consequences of delegation are addressed in this module. Participants will evaluate current behavior and determine which habits they need to develop more effectively.

◆ **Content Module 10–8: Procrastination.** This module identifies many types of procrastinating behavior, provides participants with some procrastination scenarios, and gives them strategies to overcome procrastinating self-talk.

◆ **Content Module 10–9: Interruptions and Distractions.** In this module, participants practice some techniques that deal with common "time robbers" like interruptions and other distractions.

◆ **Content Module 10–10: Managing Email.** This module focuses on one of the most common challenges in time management today: how to manage email successfully, especially in relation to other demands on our time.

◆ **Content Module 10–11: Working With Paperwork.** A critical aspect of good time management, this module shows how to handle paperwork and other clutter effectively to be organized and efficient. It also includes a wrap-up activity to help focus participants on an organization action plan.

Content Module 10–1: Participant Introductions

To help create a collaborative learning environment, this module introduces participants to each other and suggests that each person's role is to contribute to the learning process.

TIME

- 10 minutes, plus approximately 3 minutes per participant

MATERIALS

None

AGENDA

- Discuss key points. (5 minutes)

- Facilitate introduction exercise. (3 minutes per participant)

- Review some of the strengths and learning priorities of participants. (5 minutes)

KEY POINTS

- Each person has strengths in time management, and each person can contribute to learning.

- One person's development needs are often another person's strengths.

INTRODUCTION EXERCISE

The facilitator can use a variety of introduction techniques, based on the time available and his or her preference. One good technique is to have each participant in the room share information with the other participants, identifying what each one has in common with the others. At the end of each participant's introduction, ask for a show of hands to indicate who has at least one thing in common with that person regarding his or her time management skills. Then, from this group, ask for a few volunteers to share their common items. Information in the introductions should include

- Name

- Job or area in which the participant works

- How long the participant has been in that role or with the organization

- One thing the participant does well in time management

- One thing the participant would like to learn about being a more effective time manager

Content Module 10–2: Time Management Defined

The phrase *time management* may be ambiguous for some people. This module clarifies what it means to manage time, the importance of recognizing good time management, and how to identify and avoid common time wasters.

TIME

+ 1 hour, 30 minutes

MATERIALS

+ Structured Experience 12–1: Time Management Buddies (chapter 12)

+ Structured Experience 12–2: A Waste of Time (chapter 12)

+ PowerPoint presentation: *Time Management Defined.ppt* (on the website)

AGENDA

+ Lead group through the first discussion question below. (5 minutes)

+ Facilitate Structured Experience 12–1: Time Management Buddies. (30 minutes)

+ Discuss key points. (5 minutes)

+ Review the PowerPoint presentation "Time Management Defined." (20 minutes)

Discussion questions 2 and 3 are included in the presentation.

+ Facilitate Structured Experience 12–2: A Waste of Time. (30 minutes)

KEY POINTS

+ Time management requires an understanding of how to use time to achieve desired results, as well as how to use organizational tools for greater efficiency.

+ For good time management, it's important to make conscious choices about activities, and it's often necessary to limit activities to increase productivity.

+ The reasons for good time management include improving work-life balance, lowering stress levels, focusing on what's important, and achieving goals.

◆ Many of us succumb to certain "time wasters" in any given day. To manage time well, it's necessary to put a lot of energy into the process and eliminate factors that may interfere.

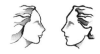

DISCUSSION QUESTIONS

1. What does time management mean to you?

2. The average adult spends 50–70 percent of the workday dealing with paper. What implications does this have for time management?

3. Time is the coin of your life. It is the only coin you have, and only you can determine how it will be spent. How do you interpret this idea?

Content Module 10–3: Time Management Self-Assessment

This module uses a self-assessment instrument to help participants identify areas in which their learning can have the most impact. It also provides an action plan for learners to identify steps they can take to improve their time management skills.

TIME

- ◆ 1 hour

MATERIALS

- ◆ Assessment 11–2: Time Management Self-Assessment (chapter 11)

AGENDA

- ◆ Discuss key points. (5 minutes)

- ◆ Administer the assessment and have participants review the "Why These Behaviors Are Important" section. (15 minutes)

- ◆ Ask participants to choose a partner and help each other complete the self-improvement plan section. (20 minutes)

- ◆ Lead entire group through discussion questions. (20 minutes)

KEY POINTS

- ◆ Effective time managers have clearly defined behaviors, which includes the ability to plan, set clear priorities, delegate, and handle distractions.

- ◆ It's important to identify which time management behaviors you use at work and at home, and adjust them as necessary.

- ◆ Knowledge of your time management strengths and weaknesses will help you be more productive and effective.

DISCUSSION QUESTIONS

1. How can the strengths that you identified in the self-assessment help you be an effective time manager? (Ask for examples from past experiences.)

2. What can you do specifically to improve in your areas of weakness?

Content Module 10–4: The Time Management Process

In this module, a five-step process for effective time management includes suggested ways to set priorities and analyze how time is currently spent, as well as strategies to filter information and handle demands on our time as they are presented.

TIME

◆ 2 hours

MATERIALS

◆ Structured Experience 12–3: Roles and Responsibilities (chapter 12)

◆ Structured Experience 12–4: Where Does the Time Go? (chapter 12)

◆ PowerPoint presentation: *The Time Management Process.ppt* (on the website)

AGENDA

◆ Lead group through discussion question 1. (5 minutes)

◆ Review the first six slides in the PowerPoint presentation "The Time Management Process." (5 minutes)

◆ Facilitate Structured Experience 12–3: Roles and Responsibilities. (45 minutes)

◆ Review the remaining slides in the PowerPoint presentation "The Time Management Process." (15 minutes)

◆ Discuss the key points. Lead participants through discussion questions 2 and 3. (10 minutes)

◆ Facilitate Structured Experience 12–4: Where Does the Time Go? (40 minutes)

KEY POINTS

◆ Time management is a five-step process that includes everything from setting priorities to scheduling and executing good time management techniques.

- It helps to take a close look at how we currently spend our time to understand areas in which we spend too much or too little time; it also provides focus for making the most of the time we have.

- We should spend the majority of our time each day on activities that are urgent and important, as well as on activities that help us achieve long-term goals and complete projects.

- It's important to recognize when we need to say "no" and be willing to manage ourselves in relation to time; these critical skills will lead to time management success.

DISCUSSION QUESTIONS

1. What are some needs that you think can be fulfilled when we engage in effective time management?

2. Why is it important to have a process for managing our time?

3. What are some techniques that you use to help you schedule your time that haven't already been discussed?

Content Module 10–5: Goal-Setting

This module explains techniques that will help set and achieve goals and identify priorities to gain focus.

TIME

◆ 1 hour, 30 minutes

MATERIALS

◆ Training Instrument 11–1: Goal-Setting Worksheet (chapter 11)

◆ Structured Experience 12–5: Goal-Setting Practice (chapter 12)

◆ PowerPoint presentation: *Goal-Setting.ppt* (on the website)

AGENDA

◆ Lead group through discussion question 1. (5 minutes)

◆ Review the PowerPoint presentation "Goal-Setting." (25 minutes)

◆ Facilitate Structured Experience 12–5: Goal-Setting Practice. (45 minutes)

◆ Discuss the key points. Lead participants through discussion questions 2 through 5. (15 minutes)

KEY POINTS

◆ Goals help us set priorities in our lives and give us direction to use our time more effectively. They also provide us with a sense of accomplishment.

◆ Three types of goals serve different purposes and needs: critical goals, enabling goals, and nice-to-have goals.

◆ The more specific and realistic we make our goals (which includes setting a timeframe for accomplishment), the more likely we are to achieve them.

♦ Goal-setting is a six-step process. Some of these steps include thinking about our roles, deciding long-term goals, breaking goals down into pieces, and scheduling those pieces.

♦ Individual work-related goals should always be consistent with department or team goals and those of the entire organization.

DISCUSSION QUESTIONS

1. What are some previous experiences you've had with goal-setting? What worked well? What was challenging for you?

2. What role does goal-setting play in your work? What process does your organization use to set goals?

3. How would working toward specific, achievable goals affect your time management?

4. How can you help others set and achieve their goals?

5. Have you encountered other models for goal-setting? If yes, what are they, and how do they compare with the process you've just practiced?

Content Module 10–6: Scheduling Time and Tasks

This module helps participants understand some of the tools available for scheduling, and it provides tips to help plan when tasks will be completed.

TIME

◆ 1 hour, 15 minutes

MATERIALS

◆ Training Instrument 11–2: Scheduling Sheet for each participant

◆ Structured Experience 12–6: Getting Around to It (chapter 12)

◆ PowerPoint presentation: *Scheduling Time and Tasks.ppt* (on the website)

AGENDA

◆ Review the PowerPoint presentation "Scheduling Time and Tasks." (15 minutes)

◆ Facilitate Structured Experience 12–6: Getting Around to It. (50 minutes)

◆ Discuss the key points. Lead the participants through the discussion questions. (10 minutes)

KEY POINTS

◆ To improve work flow and increase efficiency, group or "chunk" similar tasks together, such as returning phone calls and writing memos.

◆ To increase the accuracy of your schedule and avoid over-booking, calculate how long it takes to do certain tasks.

◆ To be effective when working on large projects, begin with the deadline, then work backwards to block off time periods on your calendar to work on the project pieces.

♦ To make a habit of scheduling, plan at the same time every day or week, and use a system to set priorities and indicate which tasks are the most important.

DISCUSSION QUESTIONS

1. What challenges do you face when you plan your days? How will you overcome them?

2. What specific tools do you currently use for scheduling your time? How effectively do they meet your needs?

3. What are some additional planning tips that have not already been discussed that you or others have found to be successful?

Content Module 10–7: Effective Delegation

Positive and negative consequences of delegation are addressed in this module. Participants will evaluate current behavior and determine which habits they need to develop more effectively.

TIME

◆ 1 hour, 15 minutes

MATERIALS

◆ Structured Experience 12-7: Delightful Delegating (chapter 12)

◆ PowerPoint presentation: *Effective Delegation.ppt* (on the website)

AGENDA

◆ Lead group through the first discussion question below. (5 minutes)

◆ Review the PowerPoint presentation "Effective Delegation." (15 minutes)

◆ Facilitate Structured Experience 12–7: Delightful Delegating. (40 minutes)

◆ Discuss key points. Lead the group through the remaining discussion questions. (15 minutes)

KEY POINTS

◆ Delegation can reduce personal stress levels, promote trust and teamwork, and provide professional growth for employees.

◆ Analysis of our own and others' behavior will help us determine whether we need to improve our delegating skills and let go of certain tasks to make more time for our priorities.

◆ Delegation of work with clearly set expectations for completion and specific progress checks will lead to success.

◆ Try to ensure that the work to be done matches the strengths and skills of the person you are delegating to, and vary the tasks delegated to any one person.

◆ Conduct a brief postwork review to set employees up for further success and help identify areas where ongoing coaching may be necessary.

DISCUSSION QUESTIONS

1. What experiences with delegation have you had or observed that did not turn out well? What happened that caused this outcome?

2. Think about someone you know who you consider to be good at delegation. What behavior does he or she exhibit that works well?

3. Describe an occasion in which you had work delegated to you. Were the expectations clear? Why or why not?

4. What are some reasons you may have hesitated to delegate in the past? What will be some specific benefits of delegating that can have an immediate impact on your life at work?

Content Module 10–8: Procrastination

This module identifies many types of procrastinating behaviors, provides participants with some procrastination scenarios, and gives them strategies to overcome procrastinating self-talk.

TIME

- ◆ 1 hour

MATERIALS

- ◆ Handout 12–1: Procrastinating Phrases for all participants

- ◆ Structured Experience 12–8: Excuses, Excuses (chapter 12)

- ◆ PowerPoint presentation: *Procrastination.ppt* (on the website)

AGENDA

- ◆ Review the PowerPoint presentation "Procrastination." (10 minutes)

- ◆ Facilitate Structured Experience 12–8: Excuses, Excuses. (35 minutes)

- ◆ Discuss the key points. Lead the participants through the discussion questions. (15 minutes)

KEY POINTS

- ◆ People procrastinate for many reasons, including a fear of failure, not knowing where to start, allowing distractions that interfere with focus, or avoidance of unpleasant tasks.

- ◆ Procrastination is a habit that's developed over time, and we need to change our self-talk and behavior to break the cycle.

- ◆ A variety of strategies decrease procrastination, including breaking large tasks into smaller ones, rewarding ourselves for accomplishing tasks, sharing progress with others, and minimizing distractions.

- ◆ If we are to improve our procrastination habit, we must commit to it.

DISCUSSION QUESTIONS

1. What impact, if any, has procrastination had on your life? Is there ever a time when procrastinating can be beneficial? If so, when?

2. Describe a specific occasion in which you or someone else procrastinated on a project. What was the outcome? What was the underlying reason for procrastination?

3. What could you do specifically to coach a procrastinator to help him or her be more effective?

4. What is the first step you will personally take to eliminate procrastination?

5. What are some rewards you would give yourself to accomplish tasks and avoid procrastination?

Content Module 10-9: Interruptions and Distractions

In this module, participants practice some techniques that deal with common "time robbers," such as interruptions and other distractions.

TIME

♦ 1 hour, 30 minutes

MATERIALS

♦ Assessment 11-7: Interruptions Self-Assessment (chapter 11)

♦ Handout 12-2: Interruption Role-Play Scenarios (chapter 12)

♦ Structured Experience 12-9: Interruption Role Play (chapter 12)

♦ PowerPoint presentation: *Interruptions and Distractions.ppt* (on the website)

AGENDA

♦ Administer Assessment 11-7: Interruptions Self-Assessment, and discuss the participants' analysis of their behaviors and their reactions. (15 minutes)

♦ Review the PowerPoint presentation "Interruptions and Distractions." (20 minutes)

♦ Facilitate Structured Experience 12-9: Interruption Role Play. (45 minutes)

♦ Discuss the key points. Lead the participants through the discussion questions. (10 minutes)

KEY POINTS

♦ Some of the ways people can get distracted from focusing on what's important include unscheduled visitors, phone calls, email, and being tired or stressed.

◆ Inform others of your workflow and availability to set expectations; this can help you take more control of your time and reduce interruptions.

◆ Suggest a specific time to get back to people when you are interrupted to maintain your focus as much as possible.

◆ Say "No," and make good use of electronic and other tools to help cut down on distractions.

DISCUSSION QUESTIONS

1. What are some techniques that you have personally used to cut down on distractions in the workplace?

2. What is an example of a situation in which you successfully handled an interruption?

3. What immediate concerns do you have about saying "No" to others? What is an approach you will try?

4. What are the primary distractions in your work environment that consistently interfere with your time management? How will you now minimize these?

Content Module 10–10: Managing Email

This module focuses on one of the most common challenges in time management today: how to successfully manage email, especially in relation to other demands on our time.

TIME

◆ 1 hour, 15 minutes

MATERIALS

◆ Handout 12–3: Subject Line Practice (chapter 12)

◆ Structured Experience 12–10: Super Subject Lines (chapter 12)

◆ PowerPoint presentation: *Managing Email.ppt* (on the website)

AGENDA

◆ Lead group through the first discussion question below. (5 minutes)

◆ Review the PowerPoint Presentation "Managing Email." (25 minutes)

◆ Facilitate Structured Experience 12–10: Super Subject Lines (35 minutes)

◆ Discuss the key points. Lead the participants through the discussion questions. (10 minutes)

KEY POINTS

◆ For maximum productivity, it is best to check and work on email no more than two or three times per day, and to take action on each email by either replying to it, filing it, or deleting it.

◆ Email replies should be short and to the point.

◆ Follow good email etiquette to model it for others and improve efficiency and clarity of communication.

◆ Only you control how you handle email. Set expectations with others on when you process email, use rules, and use automatic replies to save time.

DISCUSSION QUESTIONS

1. What are some challenges you face when it comes to managing your email?

2. What strategies do you currently use for email management? Which of the ones discussed here will you try?

3. Think back to a situation when you could have communicated better via email. How would you handle it differently today?

4. Why would some people hesitate to check their email only at certain times of the day? What can be done specifically to start to limit checking and processing email?

Content Module 10–11: Working With Paperwork

A critical aspect of good time management, this module shows how effective handling of paperwork and other clutter will help in becoming organized and efficient. It also includes a wrap-up activity to focus participants on an organization action plan.

TIME

◆ 2 hours

MATERIALS

◆ Handout 12–4: Paperwork Samples (chapter 12)

◆ Training Instrument 11–3: Organization Action Plan (chapter 11)

◆ Structured Experience 12–11: Problem Paper (chapter 12)

◆ Structured Experience 12–12: Organization Action Plan (chapter 12)

◆ PowerPoint presentation: *Working With Paperwork.ppt* (on the website)

AGENDA

◆ Review the PowerPoint presentation "Working With Paperwork." (20 minutes)

◆ Facilitate Structured Experience 12–11: Problem Paper. (45 minutes)

◆ Discuss the key points. Lead the participants through the discussion questions. (10 minutes)

◆ Facilitate Structured Experience 12–12: Organization Action Plan. (45 minutes)

KEY POINTS

- When thinking about paper and other clutter, consider whether others could find what they need on your desk, and whether the items are really as accessible as you think.

- The three-step process to deal with paper includes sorting, taking action, and maintaining a routine.

- It's important to sort paper quickly. Toss old items, and then handle those that warrant easy, fast replies as soon as possible.

- Focus on the importance and the likelihood that you will use the items; it will help the decision-making and filing processes go more smoothly.

DISCUSSION QUESTIONS

1. What tends to cause you trouble when managing paper?

2. When, if ever, has a lack of workspace organization gotten in your way? What happened?

3. How will you now approach your paperwork?

4. What can you specifically do to ensure that paper doesn't pile up?

◆

Assessments and Training Instruments

- ◆ Instructions for using assessments and instruments

- ◆ Assessments 11–1 through 11–7

- ◆ Training instruments 11–1 through 11–4

There are many worksheets and data-gathering instruments available to the facilitator of time management training. This chapter includes assessments and training instruments that rate relevant traits, competencies, and practices, as well as other tools to assist in the learning process.

An assessment differs from a test because the responses to the questions in an assessment are not considered right or wrong. Most of the assessments are designed to increase self-awareness; this process helps participants focus on learning objectives to which they can willingly commit.

Please note that the major consideration regarding these training instruments is usefulness, not predictive power. Although they have not been tested for reliability or validity, the instruments were designed primarily to generate data for action planning and personal commitment, as well as to promote learning about what is important.

Participants can use some of the training instruments during the actual learning process.

Assessments and Training Instruments

- **Assessment 11–1: Learning Needs Assessment Sheet.** During an interview with stakeholders in the organization, use this assessment to gather information about the needs of the learners and the client.

- **Assessment 11–2: Time Management Self-Assessment.** This self-assessment helps participants understand what is required to be a good time manager. It also helps them evaluate themselves and focus on areas for improvement during training.

- **Assessment 11–3: Needs Assessment Discussion Form.** This sheet gives participants a chance to think about issues they would like to discuss, and it provides information for the facilitator in a needs assessment focus group session.

- **Assessment 11–4: Facilitator Competencies.** As an aid to establishing learning priorities for your own development as a workshop facilitator, use this form as a self-assessment or as a follow-up questionnaire to solicit feedback from trainees, either after a session or at a later time.

- **Assessment 11–5: Time Management Skills Follow-Up Assessment.** Best used three to six months after the workshop, this survey should be used to determine how participants have changed their time management behaviors as a result of the training.

- **Assessment 11–6: Training Evaluation.** Use this form to conduct a Level 1 Smile Sheet evaluation. It allows training participants to provide reaction feedback for the workshop and the facilitator.

- **Assessment 11–7: Interruptions Self-Assessment.** The results of this self-assessment will help participants both review how adept they are at handling interruptions and distractions and analyze their own behavior when interrupting others.

- **Training Instrument 11–1: Goal-Setting Worksheet.** This instrument is used during Structured Experience 12–5: Goal-Setting Practice. It provides a framework for participants to identify steps to accomplish a long-term goal and to set a schedule for completion.

- **Training Instrument 11–2: Scheduling Sheet.** Used in Structured Experience 12–6: Getting Around to It, this worksheet helps participants schedule their time, both in terms of tasks to accomplish and types of activities to achieve a greater work-life balance.

◆ **Training Instrument 11–3: Organization Action Plan.** Used in Structured Experience 12–12: Organization Action Plan, this instrument helps participants plan specific steps to engage in effective time management behaviors. It also encourages participants to apply their learning for greater accountability.

◆ **Training Instrument 11–4: Facilitation Preparation Checklist.** This tool is designed to help the facilitator prepare for a training session by ensuring that he or she has all of the materials and equipment necessary to conduct a workshop.

Assessment 11–1
Learning Needs Assessment Sheet

Instructions: Use this form to take notes during interviews with stakeholders in the client organization to assess the needs of both learners and the organization itself. Be sure to understand the person's response to each question before you write a summary, and assure the interviewee that his or her comments will be both anonymous and confidential.

1. How do you define time management?

2. How would you assess your own time management skills?

3. In your role in the organization, how would you benefit from time management training?

4. Would training in time management benefit the organization at this time? Why or why not?

5. How would you assess the time management skills of others in the organization?

6. What specific behaviors have you observed regarding organizational skills and productivity that should be addressed in a time management course?

7. How do you prefer to receive time management training?

8. How interested are others in the organization in receiving time management training?

9. Should all the employees in the organization receive time management training or only select groups? Why?

10. How should time management training be marketed internally to draw attendees?

11. What desired results would you like to see for the organization after time management training?

12. What else can you tell me about your training needs at this time?

13. What are other factors for success that could affect time management training?

14. What questions do you have for me?

At the end of the interview, thank the person for his or her candid responses to your questions. Reassure the interviewee that the information will not be quoted by name, just combined with other participants' responses to analyze common themes. Explain that the time management training will reflect the priorities of those interviewed.

Assessment 11–2
Time Management Self-Assessment

Instructions: The purpose of this activity is to help you learn about what you need to be a good time manager and to help you create an action plan to improve your time management skills. Place a ✓ in one of the boxes to the right of each item, depending on how you see yourself today. No one will see your ratings unless you share them, so please be honest with yourself.

TIME MANAGEMENT BEHAVIOR	ALWAYS	FREQUENTLY	SOMETIMES	RARELY	NEVER
When working with time, I...					
1. Know my priorities and use them to focus.	☐	☐	☐	☐	☐
2. Schedule my week, noting important tasks.	☐	☐	☐	☐	☐
3. Use the first 5–10 minutes of the day to plan.	☐	☐	☐	☐	☐
4. Use organizational tools effectively.	☐	☐	☐	☐	☐
5. Have my calendar, tasks, and contacts in one place.	☐	☐	☐	☐	☐
6. Keep a notebook handy to capture information.	☐	☐	☐	☐	☐
7. Multitask at work.	☐	☐	☐	☐	☐
8. Make time for exercise and fitness.	☐	☐	☐	☐	☐
9. Eat lunch at my desk more often than not.	☐	☐	☐	☐	☐
10. Am late to meetings and activities.	☐	☐	☐	☐	☐
11. Take time to listen to coworkers.	☐	☐	☐	☐	☐
12. Am able to say "No" when necessary.	☐	☐	☐	☐	☐
13. Frequently feel exhausted or stressed.	☐	☐	☐	☐	☐
14. Spend a lot of time in unnecessary meetings.	☐	☐	☐	☐	☐
15. Have clear goals and a plan to achieve them.	☐	☐	☐	☐	☐
16. Know exactly where my time goes every day.	☐	☐	☐	☐	☐

continued on next page

Assessment 11–2, continued
Time Management Self-Assessment

TIME MANAGEMENT BEHAVIOR	ALWAYS	FREQUENTLY	SOMETIMES	RARELY	NEVER
17. Accurately estimate how long tasks will take.	☐	☐	☐	☐	☐
18. Have a system for prioritizing tasks.	☐	☐	☐	☐	☐
19. Delegate effectively to avoid doing everything.	☐	☐	☐	☐	☐
20. Procrastinate on large projects.	☐	☐	☐	☐	☐
21. Feel overwhelmed by email.	☐	☐	☐	☐	☐
22. Can effectively handle interruptions.	☐	☐	☐	☐	☐
23. Process email and voicemail at specific times.	☐	☐	☐	☐	☐
24. Manage paper effectively.	☐	☐	☐	☐	☐
25. Have an orderly workspace.	☐	☐	☐	☐	☐

Analysis: If you responded "always," "frequently," or "sometimes" for items 7, 9, 10, 13, 14, 20, or 21, these may be areas in which you need to improve your time management skills, especially your focus on what is important. You may also wish to address any of the remaining statements if you responded with "sometimes," "rarely," or "never," particularly for items 1, 2, 4, 12, 15, 18, and 24, which directly relate to how you plan your time and handle your days.

Study this information and the following pages to see why those 25 behaviors are important to be a good time manager. Then outline an action plan for self-improvement on the last page. Make sure it is a realistic plan to which you can fully commit yourself.

Why These Behaviors Are Important

The 25 behaviors that comprise this assessment are of particular importance if you would like to improve your time management skills. They represent areas you may need to address to become a more effective time manager. Further explanations of some of the behaviors that warrant additional emphasis follow:

◆ **Know my priorities and use them to focus.** If your priorities are unclear in both your work and home life, it will be difficult to achieve goals and make progress. Setting priorities provides direction for how you spend your time.

continued on next page

Assessment 11–2, continued
Time Management Self-Assessment

◆ **Schedule my week, noting important tasks.** If you have a good idea of your fixed appointments and important tasks during any given week, it will provide a clear picture of when time is available to work on important projects and goals.

◆ **Use organizational tools effectively.** It is important to have a personalized, mobile, and easy-to-use system to keep track of contacts, appointments, tasks, and notes for productivity and efficiency.

◆ **Keep a notebook handy to capture information.** Rather than have notes scattered in multiple locations on individual pieces of paper, use a notebook to capture important ideas, notes from meetings and conversations, or other information. This allows you to spend less time searching for vital details.

◆ **Multitask at work.** Although many people multitask and it is common to do so, we are at our best and most effective when we focus on one task at a time and fully concentrate on what needs to be done.

◆ **Take time to listen to coworkers.** Building a good relationship is critical to working well with others and getting things done. Take the time to listen to colleagues, which leads to greater trust, teamwork, and productivity.

◆ **Am able to say "no" when necessary.** Learn the art of saying "no" when appropriate; this prevents unnecessary time and energy spent on unimportant tasks or activities rather than on our priorities and goals. The more we can politely say "no," the more time we will have.

◆ **Frequently feel exhausted or stressed.** It serves no purpose to be run down and in a state of anxiety. We cannot perform at our best and be productive if we neglect our physical and mental health. Long-term thinking rather than short-term thinking will lead to greater focus and enable us to be more efficient, which will benefit ourselves and the workplace.

◆ **Have clear goals and a plan to achieve them.** Without goals to drive us, we can easily lose focus. Similarly, without goals broken down into action steps and specific timelines, there is a greater chance that we will not achieve them.

◆ **Know exactly where my time goes every day.** A log of how we spend our days and weeks gives us a clear picture of where we waste time and where there are pockets of time available. This leads to effective planning and better choices for effective time management.

◆ **Have a system for setting priorities.** Set priorities for tasks, such as with an "AC" system, which allows effective scheduling and flexibility when plans change and high-priority actions need to be taken. Lower priority tasks can be dropped when it is necessary to focus on more important items.

continued on next page

Assessment 11–2, continued

Time Management Self-Assessment

◆ **Delegate effectively to avoid doing everything.** Some who need help with their time management skills may think it is necessary to do everything themselves. More often than not, this makes them feel overwhelmed and causes them to spend time on tasks that are unimportant in relation to goals and projects. Delegating also helps subordinates take ownership of work and develop their skills.

◆ **Procrastinate on large projects.** Procrastination is one of the primary barriers to effective time management. Break project steps into smaller pieces and schedule them out to help prevent problems with deadlines; this also allows for greater productivity.

◆ **Feel overwhelmed by email.** Email is one of the greatest communication tools at our disposal, but it can sometimes be one of the hardest tools to handle. Learning how to sort, manage, and communicate effectively via email is a critical skill for good time management; it can help alleviate feelings of being out of control or bombarded with information and things to do.

◆ **Manage paper effectively.** A system for managing paper and other physical items in the office will alleviate stress and increase efficiency. It's important to know where important documents are located, both for personal productivity and for others who may need to find information when we are unavailable. Although some may think it necessary to save everything, doing so only slows down work and causes inefficiencies in time management processes.

Plan for Self-Improvement

1. In which two or three time management behaviors do you need to improve the most?

2. What steps can you take to improve these behaviors?

3. What are the first two or three steps you will take?

4. How will you measure your results and know whether you are improving your time management skills?

5. How will you personally benefit from improving your time management skills?

6. What support do you need from others to improve?

7. Who needs to know you are trying to improve your time management skills?

8. How will you share this information with him or her?

9. Which behaviors are particularly important for your work life? Which are particularly important for your home life?

10. When would you like to see noticeable improvement in your time management skills?

Assessment 11–3
Needs Assessment Discussion Form

Instructions: Use this sheet to prepare your comments for the focus group discussion. Write your first thoughts in response to each question. You may change your responses as the discussion progresses. Please do not write your name on this form. The facilitator will collect the form at the conclusion of the session.

1. How would you describe the time management skills of people in the organization?

2. What behaviors have you observed in terms of others' organizational skills?

3. What level(s) of employees do you think would benefit from time management training? Why?

4. Would you like to receive training to improve your own time management skills?

5. Do you think others in the organization would like to receive time management training?

6. What challenges or roadblocks may be present in the organization that could affect the success of a time management training session?

7. What would you personally like to see included in a time management training session?

8. How would you prefer that training be offered to you? (circle one)

   a. Private, individual instruction

   b. Half-day group session

   c. One-day group session

   d. Multi-day group session

   e. No preference

Thank you for your cooperation in this needs assessment.

Assessment 11–4
Facilitator Competencies

This assessment instrument will help you manage your own professional development and increase the effectiveness of your time management training sessions. Training facilitators can use this instrument in the following ways:

◆ **Self-assessment.** Use the assessment to rate yourself on the five-point scale, which will generate an overall profile and help determine the competency areas that are in the greatest need of improvement.

◆ **End-of-course feedback.** Honest feedback from the training participants can lessen the possibility that facilitators deceive themselves about the 12 competencies. Trainees may not be able to rate the facilitator on all 12, so it may be necessary to ask the participants to rate only those they consider themselves qualified to address.

◆ **Observer feedback.** Facilitators may observe each other's training sessions and provide highly useful information on the 12 competencies that are crucial to be effective in conducting time management training.

◆ **Repeat ratings.** This assessment can be the basis of tracking professional growth on the competencies needed to be an effective facilitator. The repeat measure may be obtained as often as needed to gauge progress on action plans for improvement.

The Competencies

Facilitators are faced with many challenges anytime they lead a training session. Many skills are necessary to help participants meet their learning needs and to ensure that the organization achieves its desired results for the training. This assessment contains a set of 12 important competencies that effective time management training requires. Not all seasoned facilitators have expertise in all of these competencies, but they may represent learning and growth areas for almost any facilitator.

Here is a detailed explanation of the importance of each of the dozen crucial elements of facilitator competence:

◆ **Understanding adult learners:** Uses knowledge of the principles of adult learning in both designing and delivering training.

Effective facilitators are able to draw on the experiences of the learners in a training session, and then give them the applicable content and tools to engage them fully and help them see the value of the learning. It is also important to address the participants' various learning styles and provide them with opportunities to solve problems and think critically so they can work through real business issues and develop additional skills.

continued on next page

Assessment 11–4, continued
Facilitator Competencies

◆ **Presentation skills:** Presents content clearly to achieve the desired outcomes of the training. Encourages learners to generate their own answers through effectively leading group discussions.

Of all the competencies a facilitator uses during a training session, none may be more obvious than the need to have exceptional presentation skills. The facilitator's ability to present content effectively and in an entertaining way is one of the first things learners notice and is a large part of a successful workshop. The nature of adult learning makes it equally important that the facilitator is not just a talking head, but is also adept at initiating, drawing out, guiding, and summarizing information gleaned from large-group discussions during a training session. The facilitator's role is not to feed answers to learners as if they are empty vessels waiting to be filled. Rather, it is the facilitator's primary task to generate learning on the part of the participants through their own process of discovery.

◆ **Communication skills:** Expresses self well, both verbally and in writing. Understands nonverbal communication and listens effectively.

Beyond presenting information and leading discussions, it is vital for a facilitator to be highly skilled in all aspects of communication. He or she should use language that learners can understand; give clear directions for activities; involve trainees through appropriate humor, anecdotes, and examples; and build on the ideas of others. This will lead to training sessions that are engaging and highly valuable for the participants. Facilitators must also be able to listen well and attend to learners' nonverbal communication to create common meaning and mutual understanding.

◆ **Emotional intelligence:** Respects learners' viewpoints, knowledge, and experience. Recognizes and responds appropriately to others' feelings, attitudes, and concerns.

Because learners may have many different backgrounds, experience levels, and opinions in the same training sessions, facilitators must be able to handle a variety of situations and conversations well, and be sensitive to others' emotions. They must pay close attention to the dynamics in the room, be flexible enough to make immediate changes to activities during training to meet the needs of learners, and create an open and trusting learning environment. Attendees should feel comfortable expressing their opinions, asking questions, and participating in activities without fear of repercussion or disapproval. Monitoring learners' emotions during a training session also helps the facilitator gauge when it may be time to change gears if conflict arises, if discussion needs to be refocused on desired outcomes, or if there is a need to delve deeper into a topic to encourage further learning.

continued on next page

Assessment 11–4, *continued*
Facilitator Competencies

- **Training methods:** Varies instructional approaches to address different learning styles and hold learners' interest.

  All trainees have preferred learning styles, and one of the keys to effective training facilitation is to use a variety of methods to address them. Some people are more visual ("see it") learners, and others are more auditory ("hear it") or kinesthetic ("do it") learners. An effective facilitator must be familiar with a variety of training methods to tap into each participant's style(s) and maintain interest during the training session. These methods may include such activities as small-group activities, individual exercises, case studies, role plays, simulations, and games.

- **Subject matter expertise:** Possesses deep knowledge of training content and applicable experience to draw upon.

  Facilitators must have solid background knowledge of the training topic at hand and be able to share related experience to help learners connect theory to real-world scenarios. Anecdotes and other examples to illustrate how the training content relates to participants' circumstances and work can enhance the learning experience and encourage learners to apply the information and also to use the tools they have been given. It is also crucial that facilitators know their topics inside and out, so they can answer the trainees' questions and guide them toward problem-solving and skill development.

- **Questioning skills:** Asks questions in a way that stimulates learners' understanding and curiosity. Encourages critical thinking.

  An effective questioning technique works well to assess learners' understanding of training content. It also provides opportunities for them to analyze information and think critically. When learners ask questions, the facilitator is able to see where there may be confusion or a need to review concepts for better understanding. Similarly, when a facilitator asks thought-provoking questions in a way that invites participation, learners can brainstorm solutions to problems or think about situations to help them apply the training content to the issues they deal with on a regular basis.

- **Eliciting behavior change:** Influences others effectively both individually and within groups. Gains support and commitment from others to achieve common goals and desired outcomes.

  This competency is important in two ways. First, facilitators must be able to persuade trainees to consider points of view that will lead to desired changes in behavior. A facilitator is often called upon to sell an organization's culture or policies, or to gain learners' participation to achieve the desired results of the training. To do this, a facilitator must be able to show that although he or she respects the trainees' views, the trainees must understand and accept the organization's realities and practices.

continued on next page

Second, an effective facilitator must know how to form small groups and work well with them to influence groups to accomplish tasks, work through problems, and fulfill the needs of the group members. Drawing out the creative energy of groups through brainstorming or other activities, as well as helping group members blend their unique knowledge and skills to achieve a common goal, will lead to greater commitment on behalf of the learners to improve their behavior and apply the training content.

◆ **Feedback**: Gives and receives constructive, specific, and timely feedback, and communicates observations clearly and accurately.

It is essential for facilitators to provide learners with helpful feedback, whether formally through an assessment or informally through conversation. Use specific examples to communicate a learner's strengths and weaknesses; this will help the trainee understand the information and may also increase the learner's self-reflection. It can also serve as the basis for a coaching relationship for individual training and clarify what the learner should focus on for his or her growth and development. The facilitator should also be familiar with a variety of tools to gather feedback from training participants to improve the learning experience and the facilitator's own self-reflection and growth.

◆ **Motivation**: Encourages learners to participate and achieve desired results. Generates enthusiasm and commitment from others.

It is the training facilitator's responsibility to inspire others to achieve the desired outcomes of a training session and to focus on their goals. Although it is generally believed that motivation comes from within, a skilled facilitator can unleash energy and enthusiasm by creating a vision that inspires the learners. Facilitators can provide meaningful learning activities and infuse fun into the training experience, and they must effectively channel trainees' motivation into a commitment to achieving results.

◆ **Organizational skills:** Works in an orderly and logical way to accomplish tasks. Ensures that work is correct and complete. Presents ideas logically and sequentially for learners to understand.

The importance of this competency for facilitators is twofold. First, the facilitator must have good work habits and pay attention to detail. With any training event, many factors are necessary to ensure a successful experience. Work must be done thoroughly and accurately. A well-organized training facilitator typically creates well-organized, professional training. Second, it is important for facilitators to present ideas in a logical, sequential order that allows learners to absorb new content easily and also to be able to retrieve it quickly. This also increases the probability that the learners will actually use the content. The more organized the facilitator, the better.

continued on next page

Assessment 11–4, continued
Facilitator Competencies

◆ **Time management:** Plans and uses time effectively. Balances important and urgent tasks and can work on multiple tasks simultaneously.

Facilitators do many things in addition to conducting training sessions. They must also budget their time effectively to address other priorities in their work: Prepare for the training, keep accurate records, analyze assessment data, design new content or activities, and report to the client organization. The most competent facilitators are able to multitask and keep the goals of the learners and client organization in view as much as possible. Good time management helps a facilitator keep track of all there is to do during any given day.

Facilitator Competencies

Instructions: If using this instrument as a self-assessment, place a ✓ in the box to the right of each of the 12 facilitator competencies that best describes your skill level. If using this form to provide feedback to a facilitator, place a ✓ in the box that best fits his or her level of competence in each area.

COMPETENCY	NO EXPERTISE	LITTLE EXPERTISE	SOME EXPERTISE	ADEQUATE EXPERTISE	EXPERT
Understanding adult learners: Uses knowledge of the principles of adult learning when both designing and delivering training.	☐	☐	☐	☐	☐
Presentation skills: Presents content clearly to achieve the desired outcomes of the training. Encourages learners to generate their own answers through effectively leading group discussions.	☐	☐	☐	☐	☐
Communication skills: Expresses self well, verbally and in writing. Understands nonverbal communication and listens effectively.	☐	☐	☐	☐	☐
Emotional intelligence: Respects learners' viewpoints, knowledge, and experience. Recognizes and responds appropriately to others' feelings, attitudes, and concerns.	☐	☐	☐	☐	☐

continued on next page

Assessment 11–4, continued
Facilitator Competencies

COMPETENCY	NO EXPERTISE	LITTLE EXPERTISE	SOME EXPERTISE	ADEQUATE EXPERTISE	EXPERT
Training methods: Varies instructional approaches to address different learning styles and hold learners' interest.	☐	☐	☐	☐	☐
Subject matter expertise: Possesses deep knowledge of training content and applicable experience to draw upon.	☐	☐	☐	☐	☐
Questioning skills: Asks questions in a way that stimulates learners' understanding and curiosity. Encourages critical thinking.	☐	☐	☐	☐	☐
Eliciting behavior change: Influences others effectively, both individually and within groups. Gains support and commitment from others to achieve common goals and desired outcomes.	☐	☐	☐	☐	☐
Feedback: Gives and receives constructive, specific, and timely feedback and communicates observations clearly and accurately.	☐	☐	☐	☐	☐
Motivation: Encourages learners to participate and achieve desired results. Generates enthusiasm and commitment from others.	☐	☐	☐	☐	☐
Organizational skills: Works in an orderly and logical way to accomplish tasks. Ensures work is correct and complete. Presents ideas logically and sequentially for learners to understand.	☐	☐	☐	☐	☐
Time management: Plans time effectively. Balances important and urgent tasks and can work on multiple tasks simultaneously.	☐	☐	☐	☐	☐

Assessment 11–5
Time Management Skills Follow-Up Assessment

Instructions: This form focuses on the outcomes of the training in which the learner recently participated. Please give your open and honest assessment of the person's current level of functioning. On the line to the left, write a number from 1 to 6 that best corresponds to the scale below to rate the person on some of the more important behaviors in being a good time manager.

Participant Code:
_____

1 = HIGHLY INEFFECTIVE   4 = SOMEWHAT EFFECTIVE

2 = INEFFECTIVE   5 = EFFECTIVE

3 = SOMEWHAT INEFFECIVE   6 = HIGHLY EFFECTIVE

The listener...

_____ Uses organizational tools (such as personal digital assistant, planner, and software) effectively.

_____ Appears to keep important projects on track.

_____ Has stated goals to accomplish and steps to achieve them.

_____ Takes time to listen to coworkers and build relationships.

_____ Keeps notes from meetings and conversations in one place.

_____ Sets expectations with others for responding to email and voicemail.

_____ Completes tasks in a timely manner.

_____ Goes calmly about the day without rushing from place to place.

_____ Is on time for meetings and other activities.

_____ Appears to be less stressed or tired at work.

_____ Handles interruptions and distractions well.

_____ Delegates tasks effectively and appropriately.

Assessment 11–6
Training Evaluation

Your Name: _____ Date: _____

Workshop Title: _____

Facilitator: _____ Location: _____

Please circle the number that best corresponds to your ratings for today's training session.

ITEM	POOR	FAIR	GOOD	EXCELLENT
1. Quality of the workshop content	1	2	3	4
2. Applicability of content to my work	1	2	3	4
3. Quality of training materials or handouts	1	2	3	4
4. Quality of audiovisual materials	1	2	3	4
5. Facilitator's presentation skills	1	2	3	4
6. Facilitator's knowledge of subject	1	2	3	4
7. Amount of participant interaction	1	2	3	4
8. Time allotted for activities	1	2	3	4
9. Facility or location	1	2	3	4
10. Overall workshop rating	1	2	3	4

Would you recommend this session to a colleague? Why or why not? _____

_____

How will you begin to apply the training content after today's session? _____

_____

Assessment 11–7

Interruptions Self-Assessment

Instructions: Use this assessment to evaluate the way you handle interruptions and distractions and also to determine areas for improvement. Place a ✓ in one of the boxes to the right of each item. Please complete the assessment honestly, based on how you tend to behave right now. (No one will see the results unless you choose to share them.)

DISTRACTION BEHAVIORS	TO A GREAT EXTENT	FOR THE MOST PART	TO SOME EXTENT	NOT AT ALL
When handling interruptions, I...				
1. Specify a time to get back to the interrupter.	☐	☐	☐	☐
2. Remove myself from the distracting environment.	☐	☐	☐	☐
3. Notify others when I cannot be disturbed.	☐	☐	☐	☐
4. Block off time to work on priorities.	☐	☐	☐	☐
5. Send calls to voicemail when I must focus.	☐	☐	☐	☐
6. Close out of email or turn off the pop-up box.	☐	☐	☐	☐
7. Avoid unnecessary meetings and events.	☐	☐	☐	☐
When interrupting others, I...				
8. Am mindful of their mood and demeanor.	☐	☐	☐	☐
9. Leave a voicemail or note if they look busy.	☐	☐	☐	☐
10. Avoid sitting with them for long periods of time.	☐	☐	☐	☐
11. Keep conversations concise and to the point.	☐	☐	☐	☐
12. Ask if they are available and, if not, when they will be.	☐	☐	☐	☐
13. Am mindful if they ask not to be disturbed.	☐	☐	☐	☐
14. Keep personal conversations to a minimum.	☐	☐	☐	☐

continued on next page

Assessment 11–7, continued
Interruptions Self-Assessment

Analysis: The results of this assessment can help identify areas of improvement for handling interruptions and distractions more effectively. You may find that you score higher when you prevent interruptions from seriously affecting your work than when you interrupt others, or you may score higher on particular items in either category.

For preventing interruptions from negatively affecting your work, if you rated yourself in the "To Some Extent" or "Not At All" areas for items 1, 3, 5, or 7, this means that you need to pay particular attention to setting expectations with others regarding your availability. If you scored low on items 2, 4, or 6, you may need to improve on setting the stage for greater focus on what is important.

Under interrupting others, ratings in the "To Some Extent" or "Not At All" areas for items 8–14 indicate a need to be more conscious of your own interrupting behaviors and the impact they have on others' productivity, as well as a need to pay attention to others' moods and reactions. This will lead to better working relationships and more efficiency.

Training Instrument 11–1

Goal-Setting Worksheet, for Goal-Setting Practice (Structured Experience 12–5)

Goal: _____

_____

Life Category: _____

_____

Deadline: _____

_____

Action Step 1: _____

Task 1:

Task 2:

Task 3:

Task 4:

Action Step 2: _____

Task 1:

Task 2:

Task 3:

Task 4:

Action Step 3: _____

Task 1:

Task 2:

Task 3:

Task 4:

Training Instrument 11–2

Scheduling Sheet, for Getting Around to It (Structured Experience 12–6)

SCHEDULE FOR WEEK OF _____

Time	Monday	Tuesday	Wednesday	Thursday	Friday
7:00 a.m.					
8:00 a.m.					
9:00 a.m.					
10:00 a.m.					
11:00 a.m.					
12:00 p.m.					
1:00 p.m.					
2:00 p.m.					
3:00 p.m.					
4:00 p.m.					
5:00 p.m.					
6:00 p.m.					
7:00 p.m.					
8:00 p.m.					
9:00 p.m.					
10:00 p.m.					
11:00 p.m.					

continued on next page

Training Instrument 11–2, continued

Scheduling Sheet, for Getting Around to It (Structured Experience 12–6)

BALANCE FOR WEEK OF _____

Life Category	Hours
Work	
Self	
Sleep	
Meals	

Total = 168 Hours

Training Instrument 11–3

Organization Action Plan (Structured Experience 12–12)

As a result of this workshop, I commit to:

1. Engaging in the following three behaviors to improve my time management:

    A. _____

    B. _____

    C. _____

2. Setting the following deadlines to incorporate these behaviors:

Behavior	Deadline

3. Using the following three tools or techniques to improve my time management:

    A. _____

    B. _____

    C. _____

4. Setting the following deadlines to incorporate these tools and techniques:

Tool and Technique	Deadline

5. Sharing my action plan for improvement with the following three people (other than my partner for this activity):

    A. _____

    B. _____

    C. _____

continued on next page

Training Instrument 11–3, continued
Organization Action Plan (Structured Experience 12–12)

6. Setting the following deadlines to share my action plan:

Person	Deadline

Training Instrument 11–4
Facilitation Preparation Checklist

This instrument is designed to help you, as the facilitator, prepare for a training session by ensuring that you have all of the materials and equipment necessary to conduct a workshop. All pretraining activities and needed materials and tools are listed to help set you up for a successful session. Specific materials will vary based on the content modules you will be using for the training.

Pretraining Activities

☐ Reviewed learning needs assessment data to ensure effective selection of content.

☐ Read and reviewed applicable content modules and structured experiences.

☐ Read and reviewed applicable assessments and participant handouts.

☐ Reviewed all PowerPoint slides thoroughly.

☐ Prepared additional anecdotes and examples.

☐ Practiced workshop flow and exercises.

Workshop Materials and Tools

☐ Content module and structured experience instructions

☐ Content module PowerPoint slide decks

☐ LCD projector with screen

☐ Computer and cables

☐ Power strip and extension cord

☐ Participant handouts, assessments, and instruments

☐ Attendance or registration sheet or participant sign-in sheet

☐ Participant name tags and table tent cards (if applicable)

☐ Facilitator and training evaluations

☐ Writing instruments (pens, pencils, and markers)

☐ Extra paper (if participants need it)

☐ Flipchart or easel and markers (or whiteboard in training room)

☐ Masking tape to post chart paper (if paper is not self-adhesive)

continued on next page

Training Instrument 11–4, continued
Facilitation Preparation Checklist

☐ Facilitator table or podium (to hold workshop materials)

☐ Watch or other timepiece for structured experiences and workshop flow

☐ Supplemental materials for structured experiences (such as paperwork samples to sort)

☐ Toys or candy for participants at tables (optional)

☐ Facilitator's business cards (if external to the organization) to give to participants

◆

Structured Experiences

- ◆ Explanation of structured experiences

- ◆ Step-by-step instructions for using structured experiences

- ◆ Structured experiences 12–1 through 12–12

- ◆ Handouts 12–1 through 12–4

This chapter contains 12 structured experiences to assist in the learning process. A structured experience is a step-by-step design that applies adult learning principles. Each experience includes

- ◆ **Goals:** The learning outcomes that the experience is designed to achieve.

- ◆ **Materials:** A listing of all materials required to facilitate the experience.

- ◆ **Time:** Anticipated time allowances for each step of the experience. These can vary, based on the facilitator and the participants.

- ◆ **Instructions:** Step-by-step instructions to facilitate the experience.

- ◆ **Debriefing:** Suggested debriefing topics and questions. These should be modified to meet the needs of the participants.

The Structured Experiences

Each of the following designs is self-contained. Although some of the experiences are designed specifically for learning outcomes associated with the module they support, others can be used in a variety of modules that the trainer either currently uses or is developing.

Structured Experience 12–1: Time Management Buddies.   In this structured experience, participants learn about and listen to each other in pairs. They share what they learn with the group to gauge their time management skills and challenges. It is part of Content Module 10–2: Time Management Defined.

Structured Experience 12–2: A Waste of Time.   This exercise asks participants to work in small groups to identify solutions to common time wasters. It is used in Content Module 10–2: Time Management Defined.

Structured Experience 12–3: Roles and Responsibilities.   This exercise gives participants an opportunity to brainstorm and reflect on all of the roles they fulfill in their work and personal lives; it encourages them to reflect on how well they balance their responsibilities. It is used in Content Module 10–4: The Time Management Process.

Structured Experience 12–4: Where Does the Time Go?   In this exercise, participants analyze where they spend their time in a standard week. It is part of Content Module 10–4: The Time Management Process.

Structured Experience 12–5: Goal-Setting Practice.   This is a fun and engaging exercise in which participants work with a partner to discuss and clarify their goals while they practice breaking down goals into steps. It supports Content Module 10–5: Goal-Setting.

Structured Experience 12–6: Getting Around to It.   This is an exercise that enables learners to practice their scheduling skills for various blocks of time. It is part of Content Module 10–6: Scheduling Time and Tasks.

Structured Experience 12–7: Delightful Delegating.   In this interactive exercise, participants learn from the group the best ways to delegate and how they can incorporate them into their work. It supports Content Module 10–7: Effective Delegation.

Structured Experience 12–8: Excuses, Excuses.   This experience makes participants aware of excuses used during procrastination and helps them think of thoughts and language to replace the excuses. It is part of Content Module: 10–8: Procrastination.

Structured Experience 12–9: Interruption Role Play.   This entertaining exercise allows participants to have fun with role-play scenarios in which they interrupt each other, to practice techniques for handling interruptions effectively. It is used in Content Module 10–9: Interruptions and Distractions.

Structured Experience 12–10: Super Subject Lines. In this structured experience, participants create effective subject lines for filing email and practice strategies for email management. It supports Content Module 10–10: Managing Email.

Structured Experience 12–11: Problem Paper. This exercise asks learners to work in groups to sort and process various types of paper and other materials as a way to practice organizational skills. It is part of Content Module 10–11: Working With Paperwork.

Structured Experience 12–12: Organization Action Plan. In this exercise, participants develop a plan of action for how they will organize their workstations, time, and tasks, and then share their plan with others. It is used in Content Module 10–11: Working With Paperwork.

The Handouts

Four of the structured experiences in this chapter include handouts (on the website) as part of the content for the activities. Feel free to adapt these as needed.

Handout 12–1: Procrastinating Phrases. Used in Structured Experience 12–8: "Excuses, Excuses," this handout includes phrases participants need to rewrite to be more proactive and less procrastinating.

Handout 12–2: Interruption Role Play Scenarios. Part of Structured Experience 12–9: "Interruption Role Play," this handout contains three scenarios for participants to review and act out as part of a role play activity.

Handout 12–3: Subject Line Practice. Used in Structured Experience 12–10: "Super Subject Lines," this handout contains sample emails for which participants create subject lines and file folder names to practice email organization.

Handout 12–4: Paperwork Samples. Part of Structured Experience 12–11: "Problem Paper," this handout lists objects participants need to organize as part of a small-group activity.

Structured Experience 12–1: Time Management Buddies

GOALS

The goals of this experience are to

- ◆ Allow participants to interact and learn about each other.

- ◆ Gauge their time management skills in a learning environment.

MATERIALS

None

TIME

- ◆ 5 minutes for introduction and setup of the exercise

- ◆ 15 minutes for discussion in pairs

- ◆ 10 minutes for debriefing

INSTRUCTIONS

1. Divide participants into pairs. If the number of participants is uneven, form one group of three.

2. Tell participants to engage in a five-minute conversation with each other in which one partner shares information about his or her time management challenges and the other partner shares the same information for another five minutes. During each person's chance to speak, the listener may ask clarifying questions but otherwise should not talk. The listener should concentrate as much as possible on what the speaker is saying and try to remember common challenges or themes that arise. Time the exercise so participants know when to switch roles. In a group of three, the participants should rotate roles so each has a chance to share information.

3. At the end of the 10-minute discussion time, allow five minutes for the speaker and listener to share what each remembers about the other's challenges from the conversations. Provide a time update when two minutes remain.

DEBRIEFING

Ask for a handful of volunteer participants to share some of the more interesting time management challenges and facts they learned about their partner during the activity. Lead the debriefing into a discussion of how the group can learn time management skills, as well as solutions to challenges, from each other throughout the training session and incorporate them into action. (10 minutes)

Structured Experience 12–2: A Waste of Time

GOALS

The goals of this experience are to

- ◆ Reinforce the idea that typical time wasters can interfere with productivity.

- ◆ Help participants focus their attention on how they can stop wasting time.

- ◆ Build relationships among participants.

MATERIALS

The materials needed for this structured experience are

- ◆ Writing instruments

- ◆ Blank paper for taking notes

- ◆ Whiteboard or flipchart with markers

TIME

- ◆ 5 minutes for introduction and setup

- ◆ 15 minutes for brainstorming time wasters and solutions

- ◆ 10 minutes for debriefing

INSTRUCTIONS

1. Ask participants to take out a sheet of paper and a writing instrument.

2. Divide participants into small groups, each with four or five people.

3. Explain that for the next 15 minutes their task is to discuss how they commonly waste time in a workday (for example, procrastinating, unnecessary meetings, interruptions, Internet, email, and paperwork) and brainstorm some solutions to managing time wasters. When the time is up, a spokesperson from their group will then share their solutions with the rest of the participants.

4. When ready to start timing, ask participants to think about the different roles they play at work and the activities in which they typically participate.

5. Once the 15-minute brainstorming period is over, ask the participants to begin the debriefing session. One spokesperson at a time should share the solutions from each small group.

DEBRIEFING

Ask one spokesperson per group to lead a discussion of approximately 10 minutes in which they share the solutions from the brainstorming period. Write the responses on a whiteboard or flipchart paper for the large group to see. Ask the following questions for further discussion:

1. What did you observe about when and how you waste time? Did others in your group have similar experiences?

2. What are one or two solutions that you think you can incorporate into your workday?

3. What impact do other people have on your use of time?

Structured Experience 12–3: Roles and Responsibilities

GOALS

The goals of this experience are to

- ◆ Enable participants to analyze the different roles and responsibilities in their lives.

- ◆ Teach participants the importance of balancing all of their roles and responsibilities.

- ◆ Reinforce the importance of looking at roles when setting priorities.

MATERIALS

The materials needed for this structured experience are

- ◆ Writing instruments

- ◆ Blank paper for taking notes and writing

- ◆ Whiteboard or flipchart with markers

TIME

- ◆ 10 minutes for introduction and setup

- ◆ 15 minutes to write roles and responsibilities

- ◆ 10 minutes for sharing of roles and responsibilities in pairs

- ◆ 10 minutes for debriefing

INSTRUCTIONS

1. Introduce the activity by discussing different types of roles we play in our work and personal lives (such as parent, spouse, supervisor, coworker, friend, and sibling) and share with the group specific examples of responsibilities for two or three roles of your choice (for example, role of a parent is to cook dinner, attend soccer games and teacher conferences, and help with homework). Note these roles and responsibilities on a whiteboard or flipchart paper for the group to see, and discuss how some roles may take precedence over others any given week, depending on what is of greatest importance.

2. Explain that they will have 15 minutes to think about and note up to six roles that they play at work and at home, as well as brainstorm three or four primary responsibilities they have for each role. If participants appear stuck, they can also brainstorm behaviors attached to each role (if responsibilities are vague).

3. When time is up, ask the participants to find a partner (a trio is fine if there is an odd number of learners).

4. Allow approximately 10 minutes for the pairs to compare their roles and responsibilities with each other and look for common characteristics. They can then discuss how they currently balance each of their roles and the challenges they may face.

5. After the 10-minute period, begin the debriefing.

DEBRIEFING

Lead the debriefing into a discussion of how participants can look at their roles and responsibilities to help them set priorities in any time period. Emphasize that we need to devote time each week to the roles that are of highest priority in that timeframe. Ask for some volunteers to share what insights they have gained about their own work and life balance, as well as the challenges they face in this area after doing this exercise. (10 minutes)

Structured Experience 12–4: Where Does the Time Go?

GOALS

The goals of this structured experience are to

- ◆ Illustrate the importance of analyzing where and how we spend time.

- ◆ Explore options for eliminating time wasters and creating more time.

- ◆ Build understanding of the control we have over our days.

MATERIALS

The materials needed for this structured experience are

- ◆ Writing instruments

- ◆ Blank paper for taking notes and writing

- ◆ Participants' printouts of last week's calendar and task list, pages from a planner, or information on a personal digital assistant. *Note:* For this exercise, ask the attendees to bring this information with them to the workshop. You may also want to ask the participants to bring an hour-by-hour log of how they spend their time every day for one week.

TIME

- ◆ 5 minutes for introduction and setup

- ◆ 15 minutes for noting where and how time was spent last week

- ◆ 10 minutes for personal time log analysis

- ◆ 10 minutes for debriefing

INSTRUCTIONS

1. Ask the participants to take out a sheet of paper, a pen or pencil, and their agenda and calendar or time log.

2. Tell them to list categories of time on their paper, such as meetings, appointments, work on a project, finances, family time, reading, sleeping, and exercise. For the next 15 minutes, they should note how many hours they spent in each category last week. When they

have finished, they can divide each sum by 168 (the number of hours per week) to determine the percentage of time they spent on each category of their lives.

3. When the time is up, ask participants to spend the next 10 minutes considering pockets of time that are not being used, items to cut from their days, whether activities took longer than they thought, whether they are more productive at certain times of the day than others, and whether they have an established routine.

4. Once the next 10-minute period has passed, begin the debriefing.

DEBRIEFING

Debrief the participants for approximately 10 minutes about their observations from their time logs and how they can use these insights to manage time more efficiently.

1. How are most of your hours spent?

2. Is your time balanced? If not, what is being neglected?

3. What surprises, if any, are there about where your time goes?

4. What patterns do you see? What throws off your schedule?

5. What value does this exercise have for managing your schedule?

Structured Experience 12–5: Goal-Setting Practice

GOALS

The goals of this experience are to

* Allow participants to set specific goals with action steps.

* Illustrate the effectiveness of sharing goals with another person.

* Demonstrate the use of a goal-setting tool for ease of planning.

MATERIALS

The materials needed for this structured experience are

* Writing instruments

* Copies of Training Instrument 11–1: Goal-Setting Worksheet for each participant

TIME

* 10 minutes for setup

* 20 minutes to work on goal steps in pairs

* 5 minutes to schedule tasks into a planning system (optional)

* 10 minutes for debriefing

INSTRUCTIONS

1. Distribute the Goal-Setting Worksheet to the participants and ask them to take out a pen or pencil.

2. Tell the participants that in a few minutes they will work with a partner on action steps for one long-term goal they have at work or at home. Before they begin, they should take five minutes to think about their roles, responsibilities, and priorities, and then write a goal on their worksheet. Remind them that a goal should be specific and achievable, with a deadline attached to it for the greatest chance of success.

3. After the five-minute period, ask the participants to find a partner to work with. Allow 10 minutes for one person to share his or her

goal with a partner and for the two of them to brainstorm two or three action steps for the goal and three or four tasks under each action step.

4. After 10 minutes, tell participants to switch and work through the same process with the other person's goal for 10 more minutes.

5. When finished, ask the participants to take out their planning and scheduling system (if available) and spend five minutes noting when they will complete the first tasks under the first action item. Emphasize that they should then complete this process on their own with the remaining tasks. *Note:* This step is optional for the exercise. If participants do not have a scheduling and planning system with them, simply state that when they get back from the workshop, they need to schedule the tasks into their planners or calendars.

6. Begin the debriefing once the time is up.

DEBRIEFING

Allow approximately 10 minutes to debrief participants on the effectiveness of breaking a goal into action steps with tasks they can schedule into their planning system. Ask them to reflect on why it is important to share their goals with another person (it leads to greater commitment and accountability for goal achievement) and ask them about the value of using a tool for goal-setting and planning.

Structured Experience 12–6: Getting Around to It

GOALS

The goals of this experience are to

- ♦ Demonstrate the process of scheduling tasks into a planning system.

- ♦ Illustrate the value of using a scheduling tool.

- ♦ Enable practice with scheduling tasks and "chunking" time.

MATERIALS

The materials needed for this structured experience are

- ♦ Writing instruments

- ♦ Copies of Training Instrument 11–2: Scheduling Sheet for each participant

TIME

- ♦ 10 minutes for setup and explanation of using Training Instrument 11–2: Scheduling Sheet

- ♦ 20 minutes for participants to schedule their week using the sheet

- ♦ 10 minutes for participants to complete their balance plan for their week

- ♦ 10 minutes for debriefing

INSTRUCTIONS

1. Distribute the Scheduling Sheet to the participants, and ask them to take out a pen or pencil.

2. Explain that their task is to review their upcoming week's appointments, meetings, projects, and their long-term goals and priorities, then schedule their week, using the map as a guide. Remind them to schedule set appointments first, then important tasks and steps toward goals and priorities, in line with realistic time estimates for each item. Allow 20 minutes for them to do this scheduling. *Note:* For this exercise, request that the attendees bring information regarding the coming week's appointments and tasks as they know

them to the workshop. If participants do not have this information, you may want to generate some sample tasks and appointments for them to use just for the exercise as an illustration of the process.

3. As participants work on their upcoming week's schedule, walk around the room to help those who need any assistance with the process.

4. Once participants have completed the schedule portion of the Scheduling Sheet, ask them to think about and complete the life balance plan portion. Allow up to 10 minutes for this.

5. When time is up, start the debriefing process.

DEBRIEFING

Take approximately 10 minutes for the debriefing.

1. What observations do they have about the exercise and using the sheet?

2. What implications does the exercise have regarding their current scheduling process?

3. How can looking at life balance improve their time management?

4. Does their plan include all of the categories they want to focus on for the week?

5. How can a schedule sheet such as this still be flexible and allow for creativity and spontaneity?

Structured Experience 12–7: Delightful Delegating

GOALS

The goals of this experience are to

- Teach participants effective delegating best practices.

- Demonstrate the power of good delegation for time management.

- Build relationships among participants.

MATERIALS

The materials needed for this structured experience are

- Writing instruments

- Blank paper for taking notes and writing

- Whiteboard or flipchart with markers

TIME

- 10 minutes for setup and brainstorming tasks to delegate

- 15 minutes for seeking best practices from others in the group

- 15 minutes for debriefing

INSTRUCTIONS

1. Ask participants to take out some paper and a pen or pencil. Explain that for the next 10 minutes they should think about and look at the tasks they need to accomplish to reach goals at work, finish projects, or complete other important work, then write down three to five tasks they can delegate to someone else.

2. When the time is up, tell the participants that they will have 15 minutes to talk with other learners in the workshop and discuss any best practices (strategies or techniques that work well) for delegating and any challenges people face to delegate effectively. They will have three timed rounds of five minutes each to seek out and talk with as many people in the group as possible to learn all the best practices and challenges they can (they should remain standing, to

move around the room and take their pen or pencil and paper with them). Start the first five-minute round. This may get noisy and a little hectic, but participants typically enjoy speaking with many different people and learning a variety of strategies from each other.

3. At the end of the first round, start round two (five minutes), and then move on to the final five-minute round.

4. When the time is up, begin the debriefing.

DEBRIEFING

Allow approximately 15 minutes for debriefing.

1. Ask participants to return to their seats when the last five-minute round is completed.

2. Lead a large-group discussion about the delegating best practices that they learned. Write these on flipchart paper or a whiteboard, for the group to see.

3. Ask the participants which of these strategies they will incorporate into their work.

4. Next, lead a large-group discussion on the challenges they learned. Write these on flipchart paper or a whiteboard for the group to see.

5. Ask what common characteristics the participants discovered among their own and the group's challenges. What will they now do to overcome them?

6. Ask for three or four volunteers to share a few tasks they will now delegate, and to explain how they will accomplish it. What will their first steps be?

Structured Experience 12–8: Excuses, Excuses

GOALS

The goals of this experience are to

- ◆ Illustrate how easy it is to engage in procrastinating self-talk.

- ◆ Enable participants to change their self-talk to be more productive.

- ◆ Share strategies for how to defeat a cycle of procrastination.

MATERIALS

Materials needed for this structured experience are

- ◆ Writing instruments

- ◆ Copies of Handout 12–1: Procrastinating Phrases for all participants

TIME

- ◆ 5 minutes for setup and to form small groups

- ◆ 20 minutes for creating alternate phrases in Handout 12–1

- ◆ 10 minutes for debriefing

INSTRUCTIONS

1. Divide participants into groups, each with four or five people.

2. Distribute copies of Handout 12–1: Procrastinating Phrases to everyone.

3. Have participants read through the statements listed on Handout 12–1 and review the examples provided. Explain that they will have approximately 20 minutes to work through and create new statements in place of the procrastinating phrases and that you will then ask for volunteers to share their changes with the large group.

4. When ready, move on to the debriefing.

DEBRIEFING

Take approximately 10 minutes to discuss the changes the small groups made to the procrastinating phrases. Work through each statement, seeking an example from each group. Then lead the debriefing into a discussion of whether they have used some of the procrastinating phrases in their own self-talk and the value of working through this exercise. How will they change their self-talk when they are tempted to procrastinate now?

Structured Experience 12–9: Interruption Role Play

GOALS

The goals of this experience are to

- ◆ Demonstrate strategies to handle interruptions.

- ◆ Practice effective conversations when interrupted.

- ◆ Have fun.

MATERIALS

The materials needed for this structured experience are

- ◆ Copies of Handout 12–2: Interruption Role-Play Scenarios for all participants

TIME

- ◆ 5 minutes for setup and to form groups

- ◆ 25 minutes for small-group interruption conversations

- ◆ 10 minutes for volunteers to practice in front of large group (optional)

- ◆ 5 minutes for debriefing

INSTRUCTIONS

1. Divide participants into groups of three people each. If necessary to have three per group, the facilitator may need to join a group and participate in the exercise.

2. Give copies of Handout 12–2: Interruption Role-Play Scenarios to all participants.

3. Ask participants to review Handout 12–2 with you, and explain that there are three different scenarios. Walk them through the scenarios in the handout and the format for the exercise. In their groups, they will have three rounds to switch off and play different roles, working through each scenario one at a time with everyone participating.

4. Give them a moment to decide who will play each role in Scenario A. They should all be prepared to provide feedback to each other at the end of each round and discuss how it went.

5. Allow the participants about two minutes to review the scenario, and decide which roles they will play and what approach they will take for the first round. When ready, begin the exercise by asking the first interrupter and "interruptee" for Scenario A to start the conversation. Emphasize that the players should remember to use the steps and tips they learned for handling interruptions and distractions to carry out the role-play conversation.

6. Time the exercise. Give the participants approximately four minutes to have their first conversations. When the time is up, ask the participants to share their observations and feedback about the role play for four to five minutes.

7. Ask the groups to move on to Scenario B and rotate characters so there is a new interruptee for the second round. Repeat the process in step 5 above with Scenario B. Follow the procedure in step 6, and move on to a third round to work with Scenario C, so each participant has played the interruptee.

8. When ready, ask participants to go back to their original seats.

LARGE-GROUP PRACTICE (OPTIONAL)

1. Ask for three volunteers to do the role play again for the large group (a trio for each of the three scenarios, building on what they learned from their small-group experience). Explain that the first round will now be re-created and that you need three people to role play the first interruption conversation again (Scenario A), but only for two to three minutes this time. Have the volunteers go to the front of the room and begin the role play.

2. When the time has passed, ask the audience to share what they observed about the conversation and thank the volunteers for their willingness to participate in front of the group.

3. When ready, ask for three new volunteers to re-create the interruption conversation in round two (Scenario B) and follow the procedures in step two above. Do the same for a round three conversation (Scenario C) with three new volunteers. *Note:* The above portion of this structured experience may not be suitable for all groups. The facilitator will need to gauge the personalities in the group and decide whether the large-group practice would be beneficial and enjoyable for the participants.

DEBRIEFING

Ask for a handful of volunteer participants to share their reactions to the exercise. Lead the debriefing into a discussion of how the participants performed as characters who needed to handle interruptions, how they used the steps and tips to handle interruptions and distractions during the experience, and whether they found the steps and tips they learned to be helpful. (10 minutes)

Structured Experience 12–10: Super Subject Lines

GOALS

The goals for this experience are to

- ◆ Provide participants with an opportunity to practice writing email subject lines.

- ◆ Illustrate the importance of the role of subject lines in good time management.

- ◆ Demonstrate the power of effective email filing techniques.

MATERIALS

The materials needed for this structured experience are

- ◆ Writing instruments

- ◆ Copies of Handout 12–3: Subject Line Practice for all participants

TIME

- ◆ 5 minutes for setup and to pair up participants

- ◆ 15 minutes for subject line rewrites and filing practice

- ◆ 5 minutes for comparison of subject lines and file folders in small groups

- ◆ 10 minutes for debriefing

INSTRUCTIONS

1. Divide participants into pairs. If the number of participants is uneven, form one group of three.

2. Give copies of Handout 12–3: Subject Line Practice to all participants.

3. Tell the participants that their task is to write effective email subject lines for the email messages provided on the handout, using a call to action or another attention-getting technique. Once the subject lines are complete, they should then create names of file folders that would be most effective for the emails. Allow 15 minutes for this

exercise. *Note:* The facilitator may also bring in and share poorly written subject lines from actual emails (with names removed for anonymity) and ask the group to rewrite these subject lines or just discuss them in a large-group format.

4. When the time is up, ask the pairs to join another pair to form a small group of four (or five if there is one trio).

5. Allow five minutes for the two pairs to share their subject lines and file folder names, see if there are similarities, and discuss what the differences are, if any.

6. Once the five-minute period has passed, ask the participants to return to their original seats.

DEBRIEFING

Take approximately 10 minutes to debrief the exercise by asking participants the following questions:

1. How can effective email subject lines help you manage your email? How can it benefit others?

2. How do you currently use email folders or an electronic filing system? How could you use your folders to be more effective?

3. How were the subject lines and folders you created similar or different from those in the other partner group?

4. If you were to reply to the first email on the handout, what would be most effective thing to say?

5. How would a call to action in a subject line affect your use of email?

Structured Experience 12–11: Problem Paper

GOALS

The goals for this experience are to

- ◆ Enable participants to practice sorting paper materials.

- ◆ Demonstrate the effectiveness of handling paperwork efficiently.

- ◆ Build relationships among participants.

MATERIALS

Materials needed for this structured experience are

- ◆ Writing instruments

- ◆ Copies of Handout 12–4: Paperwork Samples for all participants

- ◆ Materials for small groups to sort provided by the facilitator (for example, scribbled meeting notes, magazine articles, business memos, sample invoices, training handouts, party invitations, and sample reports)

- ◆ Blank slips of paper or sticky notes (four to six per group)

TIME

- ◆ 10 minutes for setup and to form small groups

- ◆ 10 minutes for decisions on paperwork on handout

- ◆ 15 minutes to sort items in groups

- ◆ 10 minutes for debriefing

INSTRUCTIONS

1. Divide participants into groups of three or four people each.

2. Give copies of Handout 12–4: Paperwork Samples to all participants.

3. Tell the participants that their group's first task is to review the items listed on the handout. Allow 10 minutes to brainstorm where the items could be stored or where information about them could be recorded for ease of finding them again if needed.

4. After the 10-minute period has passed, give each group four to six blank slips of paper or sticky notes and a stack of materials to sort. Ask the participants to make four piles with the materials: "file," "toss," "create appointment or task," and "read," and mark them with a slip of paper. Participants may create other sorting categories if they think it is necessary. Allow 15 minutes for this exercise.

5. As the groups are working, walk around the room to check on their progress and answer any questions they may have.

6. When the time is up, begin the debriefing.

DEBRIEFING

Take approximately 10 minutes to debrief the exercise around the concept that quickly sorting paperwork and other materials can help us with our time management and overall organization.

1. Review the handout by asking for volunteers to share where they would store or record the listed items.

2. Lead the debriefing into a discussion of what they observed during the sorting process. Was it easy or difficult? Did it make sense to them?

3. Ask for the groups to volunteer what items they included in their sorted stacks of materials.

4. What did they gain from doing this exercise?

Structured Experience 12-12: Organization Action Plan

GOALS

The goals for this experience are to

◆ Teach participants to use a tool to develop an action plan.

◆ Illustrate the importance of planning next steps for effective time management.

◆ Share plans with others for greater commitment and accountability.

MATERIALS

Materials needed for this structured experience are

◆ Writing instruments

◆ Copies of Training Instrument 11–3: Organization Action Plan for all participants

TIME

◆ 10 minutes for setup and explanation of planning tool

◆ 10 minutes for individual planning

◆ 15 minutes for sharing action plans

◆ 10 minutes for debriefing

INSTRUCTIONS

1. Give copies of Training Instrument 11–3: Organization Action Plan to all participants, and ask them to take out a pen or pencil.

2. Explain that in a few minutes you will ask each participant to complete this planning document individually and then share his or her plan with a partner.

3. Walk the participants through the instrument, and explain that you will use it as both a tool for accountability and scheduling. Point out that when items are in writing, there is a greater commitment to act. Feel free to share your own examples of time management behaviors and the techniques they have learned that could be in a plan.

4. Allow up to 10 minutes for the participants to complete the planning instrument.

5. When the 10-minute period has passed, ask the participants to pair up with someone (one group of three is fine if there is an odd number of learners in the workshop).

6. Give the pairs up to 15 minutes to share their action plans with each other, explaining that sharing them with other people leads to greater accountability.

7. When it appears that all pairs have finished, begin the debriefing.

DEBRIEFING

Ask for a handful of volunteer participants to share their action plans with the large group. Lead the debriefing into a discussion of the participants' reactions to the exercise, what they perceive as the value of completing an action plan, and whether they found it helpful to take the time to think about, document, and share action steps for time management. (10 minutes)

Handout 12–1
Procrastinating Phrases, for Excuses, Excuses (Structured Experience 12–8)

Examples:

Procrastinating Phrase: "There's plenty of time."
New Phrase: "Time will pass quickly, so I need to plan effectively."

Procrastinating Phrase: "Time always seems to get away from me."
New Phrase: "I control my time and schedule."

1. Procrastinating Phrase: "I'm sunk now. I should have started earlier."
   New Phrase:_____

2. Procrastinating Phrase: "I'm not going to do this to myself ever again."
   New Phrase:_____

3. Procrastinating Phrase: "I really need to start to work on this project."
   New Phrase:_____

4. Procrastinating Phrase: "What's the point? It will be late now, anyway."
   New Phrase:_____

5. Procrastinating Phrase: "No one is available to help me."
   New Phrase:_____

6. Procrastinating Phrase: "I'll wait until the team is ready to work on this."
   New Phrase:_____

7. Procrastinating Phrase: "I'll just mess it up anyway. I always do."
   New Phrase:_____

8. Procrastinating Phrase: "I'm not sure how to do everything, so I'll wait."
   New Phrase:_____

Handout 12–2

Scenario A (Round 1)

Patty is a busy manager at an architectural firm. She is working on a large design project for a top client's new office space, and she has a milestone deadline next week. Patty is concentrating heavily on her work when Claire, a newly hired associate, stops by Patty's office and sits in Patty's guest chair across from her desk to ask Patty for help with some new drawing software that the firm just began to use. Although Patty doesn't mind helping Claire, she really needs to stick to her timeline and get more steps of the project completed today and tomorrow before the weekend. Meanwhile, Jack, Patty's supervisor, calls Patty and tells her that he needs to speak with her right now about an important client issue.

Interruption role choices (select one of the characters to play):

1. Patty – Manager
2. Claire – New associate
3. Jack – Supervisor

Scenario B (Round 2)

Tim, a sales representative for a software company, needs to make an important call to follow up on a proposal he sent to the CEO of a potential new client. Tim works in a cubicle in an open office environment and often finds it hard to concentrate or have a conversation in which there needs to be some sense of privacy. Just as Tim is about to make his call, Christine, a fellow salesperson who works in the next cubicle, interrupts him to ask his opinion of the proposal she's writing for a different prospect and to see if he thinks it needs some work. Luke, Tim's boss, also stops by with a pressing new project for Tim that is quite involved; it requires Tim to investigate competing software so the company knows what it is currently up against for new sales. Luke appears to be impatient and eager for Tim to start this new project right away. Tim has not had much experience dealing with situations in which his boss brings new projects to him and wants him to drop everything else, especially when there is an important client conversation he must have.

Interruption role choices (select one of the characters to play):

1. Tim – Salesperson
2. Christine – Fellow salesperson
3. Luke – Supervisor

Scenario C (Round 3)

Kate, a call center representative with a busy department store's catalog division, is on the phone with an irate customer who has had a problem with a recent order. While Kate is on the phone, Ben, a fellow employee, stops by to go with her to the kitchen for an office party to celebrate the number of catalog sales that month. Ben repeatedly checks in on Kate's

continued on next page

Handout 12–2, continued

Interruption Role-Play Scenarios, for Interruption Role Play (Structured Experience 12–9)

call, looking irritated and anxious. Diane, Ben and Kate's friend, also drops by to see why they are not yet at the party and to ask Kate a question about a catalog item. Ben and Diane start a conversation near Kate's desk and discuss a call Ben had with a customer earlier that afternoon. It appears that Kate will be on the phone for a while.

Interruption role choices (select one of the characters to play):

1. Kate – Call center representative

2. Ben – Colleague

3. Diane – Colleague

Handout 12–3

Subject Line Practice, for Super Subject Lines (Structured Experience 12–10)

1. Subject Line: _____

Email Text: Attached are the minutes from the last board meeting. Please look these over when you have time, preferably by the next meeting on September 8. Let me know if you see anything that needs changing, and I'll make any necessary corrections. Thank you!

2. Subject Line: _____

Email Text: The annual charity auction for XYZ Foundation is coming up on November 10. Would your company consider donating a prize to put up for auction? If so, it would be great to have your participation. Last year, we raised more than $40,000 for XYZ Foundation, and 200 people attended the event. It will be downtown at the Civic Theater once again. We need all of the auction prizes in place by October 15. Thank you for your consideration.

3. Subject Line: _____

Email Text: This is a reminder that all monthly sales reports are due to me by the end of next week. It is critical that I receive your reports on time, as I need to present our team's figures to the board of directors on March 28. Let me know if you will have any problems getting your report turned in, or if there is anything you need from me to help you compile the information. Thank you for your help.

4. Subject Line: _____

Email Text: The holiday party is quickly approaching! Please read the attached invitation to see all of the details for the event. To be able to order the refreshments, we need an accurate head count, so please RSVP by December 3 at the latest. A hard copy of the invitation is also in your mailbox. One guest per employee is welcome to attend, and there are four dinner selections to meet your needs. Happy Holidays!

5. Subject Line: _____

Email Text: Hello! I have a couple of questions for you regarding the Smith account. When you have a chance, could you please let me know when you're free to talk for a few minutes? I need to get back to the client by midday tomorrow and am stuck on some items for the proposal for new business I'm putting together.

File Folder Names:

Email #1: _____

Email #2: _____

Email #3: _____

Email #4: _____

Email #5:_____

Handout 12–4
Paperwork Samples, for Problem Paperwork (Structured Experience 12–11)

How would you organize these items?

1. Notes and hard copies of materials from a monthly department meeting

   _____

2. An article on strategic planning (a long-term project) from a trade magazine

   _____

3. The first draft of a proposal a colleague left on your desk to review

   _____

4. An invitation you received through the mail to a client's open house

   _____

5. An unpaid invoice to turn in to accounting

   _____

6. Business expense receipts from attending an out-of-town conference

   _____

7. A book on leadership you've been meaning to read

   _____

8. A brochure for a seminar that would be good for your team to attend

   _____

9. Handouts from a recent training workshop you attended

   _____

10. Six sticky notes with reminders on them to call people back

   _____

◆

Using the Website

In your web browser, open the webpage www.ASTD.org/TimeManagement-Training.

DOWNLOADS

Contents of the Website

The website that accompanies this workbook on time management training contains three types of files. All of the files can be used on a variety of computer platforms.

- **Adobe.pdf documents.** These include handouts, assessments, training instruments, and training tools.

- **Microsoft Word documents.** These text files can be edited to suit the specific circumstances of organizations and to fit the precise needs of trainers and trainees.

- **Microsoft PowerPoint presentations.** These presentations add interest and depth to many of the training activities included in the workbook.

- **Microsoft PowerPoint files of overhead transparency masters.** These files make it easy to print viewgraphs and handouts in black-and-white rather than using an office copier. They contain only text and line drawings; there are no images to print in grayscale.

Computer Requirements

To read or print the .pdf files on the website, you must have Adobe Acrobat Reader software installed on your system. The program can be downloaded for free from the Adobe website, www.adobe.com.

To use or adapt the contents of the PowerPoint presentation files on the website, you must have Microsoft PowerPoint software installed on your system. If you just want to view the PowerPoint documents, you must have an appropriate viewer installed on your system. You can download various viewers for free from Microsoft's website, www.microsoft.com.

Printing From the Website

TEXT FILES

You can print the training materials using Adobe Acrobat Reader; just open the .pdf file and print as many copies as you need. The following documents can be directly printed from the website:

- ◆ Assessment 11–1: Learning Needs Assessment Sheet
- ◆ Assessment 11–2: Time Management Self-Assessment
- ◆ Assessment 11–3: Needs Assessment Discussion Form
- ◆ Assessment 11–4: Facilitator Competencies
- ◆ Assessment 11–5: Time Management Skills Follow-Up Assessment
- ◆ Assessment 11–6: Training Evaluation
- ◆ Assessment 11–7: Interruptions Self-Assessment
- ◆ Training Instrument 11–1: Goal-Setting Worksheet
- ◆ Training Instrument 11–2: Scheduling Sheet
- ◆ Training Instrument 11–3: Organization Action Plan
- ◆ Training Instrument 11–4: Facilitation Preparation Checklist
- ◆ Structured Experience 12–1: Time Management Buddies
- ◆ Structured Experience 12–2: A Waste of Time
- ◆ Structured Experience 12–3: Roles and Responsibilities
- ◆ Structured Experience 12–4: Where Does the Time Go?
- ◆ Structured Experience 12–5: Goal-Setting Practice
- ◆ Structured Experience 12–6: Getting Around to It
- ◆ Structured Experience 12–7: Delightful Delegating
- ◆ Structured Experience 12–8: Excuses, Excuses
- ◆ Structured Experience 12–9: Interruption Role Play
- ◆ Structured Experience 12–10: Super Subject Lines
- ◆ Structured Experience 12–11: Problem Paper
- ◆ Structured Experience 12–12: Organization Action Plan
- ◆ Handout 12–1: Procrastinating Phrases

◆ Handout 12–2: Interruption Role-Play Scenarios

◆ Handout 12–3: Subject Line Practice

◆ Handout 12–4: Paperwork Samples

POWERPOINT SLIDES

You can print the presentation slides directly from the website using Microsoft PowerPoint; just open the .ppt files and print as many copies as you need. You can also make handouts of the presentations by printing 2, 4, or 6 slides per page. These slides will be in color, with design elements embedded. PowerPoint also permits you to print these in grayscale or black-and-white representations. Many trainers who use personal computers to project their presentations bring along viewgraphs just in case there are glitches in the system.

Adapting the PowerPoint Slides

You can modify or otherwise customize the slides by opening and editing them in the appropriate application. You must, however, retain the denotation of the original source of the material; it is illegal to pass it off as your own work. You may indicate that a document was adapted from this workbook, written and copyrighted by Lisa J. Downs, and published by ASTD. The files will open as "Read Only," so before you adapt them you will need to save them onto your hard drive under a different filename.

Showing the PowerPoint Presentations

On the website, the following PowerPoint presentations are included:

◆ *Time Management Defined.ppt*

◆ *The Time Management Process.ppt*

◆ *Goal-Setting.ppt*

◆ *Scheduling Time and Tasks.ppt*

◆ *Effective Delegation.ppt*

◆ *Procrastination.ppt*

◆ *Interruptions and Distractions.ppt*

◆ *Managing Email.ppt*

◆ *Working With Paperwork.ppt*

Table A–1 Navigating Through a PowerPoint Presentation

KEY	POWERPOINT "SHOW" ACTION
Space bar *or* Enter *or* Mouse click	Advance through custom animations embedded in the presentation
Backspace	Back up to the last projected element of the presentation
Escape	Abort the presentation
B *or* b B *or* b *(repeat)*	Blank the screen to black Resume the presentation
W *or* w W *or* w *(repeat)*	Blank the screen to white Resume the presentation

Using the .ppt format for the presentation means that it automatically shows full-screen when you double-click on its filename. You can also open Microsoft PowerPoint and launch it from there.

Use the space bar, the enter key, or mouse clicks to advance through a show. Press the backspace key to back up. Use the escape key to exit a presentation. If you want to blank the screen to black while the group discusses a point, press the *B* key. Pressing it again restores the show. If you want to blank the screen to a white background, do the same with the *W* key. Table A-1(on p. 186) summarizes these instructions.

We strongly recommend that trainers practice making presentations before using them in training situations. You should be confident that you can cogently expand on the points featured in the presentations and discuss the methods for working through them. If you want to engage your training participants fully (rather than worry about how to show the next slide), become familiar with this simple technology before you use it. A good practice is to insert notes into the "Speaker's Notes" feature of the PowerPoint program, print them out, and have them in front of you when you present the slides.

◆

Allen, David. *Getting Things Done: The Art of Stress-Free Productivity*. New York: Penguin Group, 2001.

Bassi, Laurie J., and Russ, Darlene. *What Works: Assessment, Development, and Measurement*. Alexandria, VA: ASTD, 1997.

Bossidy, Larry, and Ram Charan. *Execution: The Discipline of Getting Things Done*. New York: Crown Business, 2002.

Carliner, Saul. *Training Design Basics*. Alexandria, VA: ASTD, 2003.

Cook, Marshall J. *Time Management: Proven Techniques for Making the Most of Your Valuable Time*. Avon, Massachusetts: Adams Media, 1998.

Covey, Stephen R. *The 7 Habits of Highly Effective People*. New York: Free Press, 2004.

Haneberg, Lisa. *Focus Like a Laser Beam: 10 Ways to Do What Matters Most*. San Francisco: Jossey-Bass, 2006.

Kemp, Jerrold E., Gary R. Morrison, and Steven M. Ross. *Designing Effective Instruction* (2nd edition). Upper Saddle River, New Jersey: Prentice-Hall, 1998.

Kirkpatrick, Donald L., and James D. Kirkpatrick. *Evaluating Training Programs: The Four Levels* (3rd edition). San Francisco: Berrett-Koehler Publishers, 2006.

Knowles, Malcolm S., Elwood F. Holton III, and Richard A. Swanson. *The Adult Learner* (5th edition). Houston, Texas: Gulf Publishing Company, 1998.

Morgenstern, Julie. *Time Management From the Inside Out* (2nd edition). New York: Henry Holt and Company, 2004.

Roberto, Michael. *Time Management: Increase Your Personal Productivity and Effectiveness.* Boston: Harvard Business School Press, 2005.

Snead, G. Lynne and Joyce Wycoff. *To Do...Doing...Done!* New York: Fireside, 1997.

Tobey, Deborah. *Needs Assessment Basics.* Alexandria, Virginia: ASTD, 2005.

Yelon, Stephen L. *Powerful Principles of Instruction.* White Plains, New York: Longman Publishers USA, 1996.

About the Author

◆

Lisa J. Downs is a leadership development manager for T-Mobile USA's Integrated Customer Experience Group, where she conducts communications, leadership, and management training and serves as a coach and curriculum developer. She is also the owner of DevelopmentWise, her consulting business in Redmond, Washington. Before this, Downs was a senior learning and organizational development specialist for The Growth Partnership, an accounting consulting firm, headquartered in St. Louis, Missouri. At The Growth Partnership, she worked as a workshop facilitator, a coach for the organization's partner development program, and a curriculum designer with an emphasis on supervisory and communications skills. Downs was also the manager of learning and development for Clark Nuber PS, a "Best of the Best" accounting firm in the Seattle area, where she was responsible for overseeing the training function and leading the learning initiatives of the firm. In addition, she established the Accounting Careers Program for the Washington Society of Certified Public Accountants.

Downs earned her secondary education teaching credentials in 1996 and taught language arts courses at the high school level, which launched her career in learning and development, training, and curriculum design. Downs has also worked for both commercial and public radio stations in the Quad-Cities area of Illinois and Iowa.

Downs received her master of science in education degree with a concentration in adult education from Western Illinois University in 2000 and completed her undergraduate degree in speech communications in 1991 at Augustana College in Rock Island, Illinois. She is the 2008 president of the American Society of Training & Development's Puget Sound chapter, after serving as its vice-president of membership for two years. Downs is an active member of national ASTD, as well as the International Society for Performance Improvement and the Seattle chapter of the Society for Human Resource Management.

Continuing her passion for education and youth development, Downs also serves as a volunteer for junior achievement and the Washington chapter of DECA, an organization that gives students hands-on experience in the fields of marketing, business, and entrepreneurship. She and her husband, Chris, moved to the Seattle area in 2000, where they live with their two cats, Gracie and Fletcher.

Downs is the author of *Listening Skills Training*, another title in the ASTD Trainer's WorkShop series.

Index

◆